W9-BXH-074

BIOLOGICAL AND CHEMICAL TERRORISM

A Guide for Healthcare Providers and First Responders

RC
88.9
.T47
W456
2003

BIOLOGICAL AND CHEMICAL TERRORISM

A Guide for Healthcare Providers and First Responders

Raymond S. Weinstein, M.D.
Ken Alibek, M.D., Ph.D., D.Sc.

Thieme

New York · Stuttgart

  KALAMAZOO VALLEY
COMMUNITY COLLEGE
LIBRARY

FEB 0 3 2005

Thieme Medical Publishers, Inc.
333 Seventh Ave.
New York, NY 10001

Editorial Assistant: Jennifer Berger
Director, Production and Manufacturing: Anne Vinnicombe
Production Editor: Becky Dille
Marketing Director: Phyllis Gold
Sales Manager: Ross Lumpkin
Chief Financial Officer: Peter van Woerden
President: Brian D. Scanlan
Compositor: Thomson Press International
Printer:

Library of Congress Cataloging-in-Publication data is available from the publisher.

Copyright © 2003 by Thieme Medical Publishers, Inc. This book, including all parts thereof, is
legally protected by copyright. Any use, exploitation or commercialization outside the narrow
limits set by copyright legislation, without the publisher's consent, is illegal and liable to prosecution.
This applies in particular to Photostat reproduction, copying, mimeographing or duplication of any
kind, translating, preparation of microfilms, and electronic data processing and storage.
Important note: Medical knowledge is ever-changing. As new research and clinical experience
broaden our knowledge, changes in treatment and drug therapy may be required. The authors
and editors of the material herein have consulted sources believed to be reliable in their efforts to
provide information that is complete and in accord with the standards accepted at the time of
publication. However, in the view of the possibility of human error by the authors, editors, or
publisher, of the work herein, or changes in medical knowledge, neither the authors, editors, or
publisher, nor any other party who has been involved in the preparation of this work, warrants that
the information contained herein is in every respect accurate or complete, and they are not
responsible for any errors or omissions or for the results obtained from use of such information.
Readers are encouraged to confirm the information contained herein with other sources. For
example, readers are advised to check the product information sheet included in the package of each
drug they plan to administer to be certain that the information contained in this publication is
accurate and that changes have not been made in the recommended dose or in the contraindications
for administration. This recommendation is of particular importance in connection with new or
infrequently used drugs. Some of the product names, patents, and registered designs referred to in
this book are in fact registered trademarks or proprietary names even though specific reference to
this fact is not always made in the text. Therefore, the appearance of a name without designation
as proprietary is not to be construed as a representation by the publisher that it is in the public
domain.

Printed in the United States of America

5 4 3 2 1

TMP ISBN 1-58890-186-6
GTV ISBN 3 13 136681 8

A Quick Reference for Potential Biological Weapons

Disease/Agent	Incubation	Initial Symptoms
Anthrax (inhalational) (Bacillus anthracis)	1–6 days	FLI[1] (includes fever or history of fever) with chest discomfort, often widened mediastinum and pleural effusions on CXR. Malaise may be profound. Followed by high fever, dry cough, severe respiratory distress, cyanosis, septicemia, and death
Botulinum toxin (Clostridium botulinum)	12–36 hr	Diplopia, photophobia, ptosis, hoarseness, slurred speech; progresses to total paralysis
Brucellosis (Brucella suis & melitensis)	Days–months	FLI,[1] back pain, arthralgias. Pneumonia or nodules on CXR
Cholera (Vibrio cholerae)	4 hr–5 days	Severe rice water diarrhea, nausea, vomiting, collapse
Ebola & Marburg viral hemorrhagic fevers	3–14 days	FLI,[1] stomach pain, diarrhea, rash, weakness, bleeding, shock
Glanders (Burkholderia mallei)	3–14 days	Sudden onset of FLI,[1] chest pain, photophobia, diarrhea, splenomegaly, pneumonia
Hantavirus pulmonary syndrome	1–5 weeks	FLI,[1] dyspnea, headache, GI symptoms. Later rales and ARDS
Lassa virus & the South American viral hemorrhagic fevers	3–19 days	Fever, malaise, myalgias, back, chest, & abdominal pain, dysesthesia, cough, vomiting, ↓BP, oliguria, hemorrhages
Plague (pneumonic) (Yersinia pestis)	1–6 days	FLI[1] with high fever, possible hemoptysis, patchy pneumonia
Q fever (Coxiella burnetii)	2–14 days	FLI,[1] may progress to atypical pneumonia &/or hepatitis
Ricin (castor bean extract) & **Abrin** (rosary pea extract)	4–8 hr	Fever, dyspnea, cough, nausea, chest tightness, arthralgias, airway necrosis &/or ARDS
Smallpox (Variola major)	3–19 days	FLI[1] with backache, possible delirium, chickenpox-like rash starting on arms.
Staphylococcal enterotoxin B	3–12 hr	FLI[1] with high fever and prostration. Severe cases produce dyspnea, chest pain, GI symptoms
T-2 (tricothecene) mycotoxins (multiple fungi)	Minutes	Eye/skin pain, burning, redness & blisters, dyspnea, wheezing, cough, N/V, bloody stools, cramping
Tularemia (pneumonic) (Francisella tularensis)	1–21 days	FLI[1] with prostration, chest pain, & hemoptysis

[1]FLI = flulike illness (fever, chills, cough, malaise, headache, sore throat, and/or myalgias).

A Quick Reference for Potential Biological Weapons

Medical Management	Contagion Risk	Infection Precautions
Prophylaxis: Doxy 100 mg Q12h PO **or** cipro 500 mg bid PO **Treatment**: Doxy 100 mg Q12h IV **or** cipro 400 mg Q12h IV (levofloxacin may be substituted) **plus** rifampin 600 mg PO qid **or** clinda 900 mg IV Q6h **or** vanco 1 g IV Q12h **or** Biaxin 500 mg PO bid **or** imipenem 500 mg IM/IV Q6h **or** ampi 500 mg IV/PO Q6h. Same drug choices in children & pregnancy, but use peds dosing in children (MMWR 10-26-01)	Very low (cutaneous only)	Standard[2]
Early administration of botulinum antitoxin is critical; supportive care including mechanical ventilation	None	Standard[2]
Treat PO with doxy 100 mg Q12h **plus** rifampin 600 mg qid PO for bioterrorism attack	None	Standard[2]
IV replacement of fluids & lytes. tetracyline 500 mg Q6h, **or** doxy 100 mg Q12h, **or** cipro 500 mg Q12h. RX × 3 days	Very low	Standard[2]
No specific treatment. Supportive care, oxygen, replace fluids, management of coagulopathy	**Moderate**	Airborne[4]
Prophylaxis: TMP-SMX DS Q12h may help **Treatment**: Severe→ceftazidime 2 g IV Q8h TMP-SMX (2 mg/kg–10 mg/kg) IV qid **or** sulfadiazine 25 mg/kg Q6h for 2 wks, then switch to PO TMP-SMX. Localized (including pulmonary)→amox-clav 20 mg/kg PO tid **or** tetracycline 13 mg/kg PO tid **or** sulfadiazine 25 mg/kg PO Q6h or TMP 2 mg/kg–SMX 10 mg/kg PO bid for 60–150 days based on clinical response	Low	Droplet[3]
Supportive care, mechanical ventilation. No specific treatment	Very low	Standard[2]
Supportive care with IV fluids, colloids, and management of coagulopathy. Ribavirin IV 30 mg/kg loading dose, then 15 mg/kg Q6h for 4 days, then 7.5 mg/kg Q8h for 6 days	**Moderate**	Airborne[4]
Streptomycin 15 mg/kg/q12h IV (gent may be used instead) **or** doxy 100 mg Q12h IV **or** cipro 400 mg Q12h IV	**Moderate to High**	Droplet[3]
Doxy 100 mg Q12h IV **or** tetra 500 mg Q6h PO. cipro 500 mg Q12h IV may also be useful	Low	Standard[2]
Supportive only: wash skin with soap and water, respiratory support/mechanical ventilator, gastric lavage, activated charcoal & mg citrate if ingested	Very low	Standard[2]
Vaccine prior to onset of illness (3–7 days); otherwise supportive care, isolation, or home quarantine	**Very high**	Airborne[4] & contact[5]
Symptomatic and supportive care with IV fluids, oxygen, &, if necessary, intubation, mechanical ventilation, PEEP	Very low	Standard[2]
Supportive; wash patient (soap & water) & remove clothes to remove toxin residue (yellow or greenish oily liquid)	Direct contact only	Standard[2]
Gent 1 mg/kg/Q8h IV **or** Cipro 400 mg Q12h IV **or** Cipro 750 mg Q12h IV **or** streptomycin 7.5–10 mg/kg/Q12h IM	Low	Standard[2]

[2]Standard precaution: gloves and frequent hand washing. For possibility of splashes of body fluid, wear gown, mask, and eye protection.
[3]Droplet precautions: standard precautions plus surgical or HEPA-filter (or equivalent) mask.
[4]Airborne precautions: isolation, negative pressure room, gloves, gown, HEPA-filter or equivalent mask, frequent hand washing.
[5]Contact precautions: standard precautions plus private room or cohorting of patients, gown, gloves, dedicated noncritical patient care equipment.

A Quick Reference for Chemical Weapons

Agent	Source[5]	Onset	Initial Symptoms
Nerve agents—Sarin (GB), soman (GD), tabun (GA), VX (liquid, vapor, aerosol)	WMD	Vapor/aerosol—seconds to minutes Liquid—minutes to hours	Miosis, salivation, rhinorrhea, sweating, wheezing and chest tightness, dyspnea, abdominal cramping, diarrhea, muscle fasciculations, spasms, twitching, paralysis, coma, seizures
Vesicants—mustard, lewisite, phosgene oxime (vapor, liquid)	WMD, I/M	Minutes to hours	Burning/itching/stinging of skin w/ erythema & blisters; redness, tearing and burning of eyes, lid spasm, photophobia; nasal irritation & bleeding, sore throat, laryngitis, productive cough
Pulmonary agents—chlorine, phosgene, diphosgene, PFIB (gas)	WMD, I/M	Minutes to hours	Eye, nasal, and oral pain and irritation, tearing, cough, substernal ache &/or pressure. Progresses to dyspnea, choking, rales, hemoptysis, pulmonary edema
Lacrimators (tear gas)—CN, CR, CS (particulate solid, mist, smoke)	WMD	Seconds	Eye tearing, redness and lid spasm; burning and pain of eyes, nose, mouth, and throat; sneezing, salivation, chest tightness, and cough. **Unlike pulmonary agents and vesicants, onset is immediate and symptoms improve over 15–30 min following termination of exposure.**
Cyanide—hydrogen cyanide, cyanogens (vapor, liquid)	WMD, I/M	Seconds to minutes	Flushing, giddiness, sweating, headache, confusion, gasping, seizure, coma, respiratory arrest, cardiac arrest. Cyanosis is rare.
Arsine (AsH$_2$) (gas)	I/M	2–24 hr	Nausea, vomiting, crampy abdominal pain, malaise, dizziness, headache, dyspnea, RBC hemolysis, anemia, ↑K, ↓Ca, hypotension, hemoglobinuria, renal failure. Occasionally delirium.
Anhydrous ammonia (NH$_3$), **hydrochloric acid** (HCl), **sulfur dioxide** (SO$_2$) (gas, mist, liquid)	I/M A	Seconds to minutes	Eye, nasal, oral, & upper airway irritation/burns; pain, hoarseness; possible stridor, cough, & wheezing. ↑ concentration &/or ↑ exposure can act like pulmonary agents
Hydrofluoric acid (HF) (liquid, vapor, aerosol)	I/M	Seconds to days	Initial same as anhydrous ammonia, plus later deep skin burns, ↓Ca, ↓Mg, ↑K, tetany, arrhythmias, CHF, shock, death (serious systemic effects may take days to occur)
Hydrogen sulfide (H$_2$S) (gas)	I/M	Minutes	Eye, nasal, oral, and upper airway irritation and pain, skin erythema, flushing, sweating, headache, nausea, vomiting, gasping, tachypnea, possible wheezing, rales, & pulmonary edema. High doses rapid apnea, coma, death

[1] Each military **Mark 1** kit contains atropine 2 mg and 2-PAMCI 600 mg in separate autoinjectors.
[2] Assumes absent or incomplete decontamination prior to hospital. In fully decontaminated patients, use only standard precautions.
[3] Standard precautions: gloves and frequent hand washing. For possibility of splashes of fluids, wear gown, mask, and eye protection
[4] Respirator: full face with organic vapor filters, PAPR or self-contained breathing apparatus
[5] Sources of agents: I/M = industrial/manufacturing, A = agriculture, WMD = weapon of mass destruction
[6] peds = pediatric medication dosage

A Quick Reference for Chemical Weapons

Initial Medical Management	Contact Risk	Precautions
Atropine 2–6 mg (peds 0.02 µg/kg) IM/IV + **pralidoxime Cl (2–PAMCL)** 600–2000 mg (peds 20 mg/kg) IM/IV[1]; repeat atropine 2–4 mg & 2-PAMCL 600–1000 mg Q2–5 min PRN; **Diazepam** 10 mg (peds 0.1–0.3 mg/kg) slow IVP prn seizure mechanical ventilator prn; remove any residual agent from skin with soap & water or 1 part bleach in 9 parts water	High.[2] Avoid contact with residual liquid agent, or inhalation of fumes trapped in patient clothing.	Maximum available protection,[2] including respirator[4]
Remove residual agent with 1 part bleach in 9 parts water and rinse with copious water. Supportive care. In **lewisite use BAL** in oil 4 mg deep IM Q4h × 3 doses (Q2h in severe poisoning). **Limit IV fluids.** Systemic analgesics. Treatment of blisters and skin lesions as in thermal burns.	Low. Avoid contact with agent or inhalation of fumes.	Maximum available protection,[2] respirator[4]
Supportive with IV fluids, O_2, manage airway secretions, intubation, PEEP, observation for at least 24 hr.	Low to none	Standard[3]
No specific treatment is required. Patients should be decontaminated with 1 part bleach in 9 parts water, or soap and water. Flush eyes with saline or water.	Low	Standard[3]
100% O_2, CPR, intubation & mechanical ventilation, **amyl nitrite** via inhalation Q3 min until IV access, then **3% sodium nitrite** 10 ml (peds 0.2 mg/kg in 3% solution) IV over 5 min, followed by **25% Na sodium thiosulfate** 50 ml (peds 1.65 mg/kg in 25% solution) IV over 10 min. Inject each over 3–5 min. May repeat $\frac{1}{2}$ dose of each in 30 min if needed.	Low to none. Avoid contact with victim's wet clothing.[2]	Standard[3]
No specific treatment or antidote. Chelation does not help. Avoid fluid overload in case of renal failure. Consider exchange transfusion.	Low to none	Standard[3]
Supportive care; thoroughly rinse victim if not already done; stabilize/protect airway & manage secretions; O_2; early intubation if needed, mechanical ventilation & PEEP if necessary; observation for at least 24 hr after exposure	Low to none. Avoid contact with residual liquid.	Standard[3]
Supportive care; rapid decontamination (H_2O) if not already done; stabilize/protect airway & manage secretions; O_2; closely follow & correct lyte imbalances; cover burns w/**2.5 gms Ca gluconate in 100 ml K-Y Jelly**. Avoid emesis. **1.5 ml of 10% Ca gluconate in 4.5 ml NS** via nebulizer inhalation.	Low. Avoid contact with residual liquid or contaminated clothing	Standard,[3] double glove & eye protection if residual liquid
100% O_2, **CPR**, intubation & mechanical ventilation if needed. **Sodium bicarbonate** ($NaHCO_3$) by IV infusion may be helpful. **Sodium Nitrite** 10 ml (peds 0.2 mg/kg in 3% solution) IV over 5 min.	Low to none	Standard[3]

[1] Each military **Mark 1** kit contains atropine 2 mg and 2-PAMCl 600 mg in separate autoinjectors.

[2] Assumes absent or incomplete decontamination prior to hospital. In fully decontaminated patients, use only standard precautions.

[3] Standard precautions: gloves and frequent hand washing. For possibility of splashes of fluids, wear gown, mask, and eye protection

[4] Respirator: full face with organic vapor filters, PAPR or self-contained breathing apparatus

[5] Sources of agents: I/M = industrial/manufacturing, A = agriculture, WMD = weapon of mass destruction

[6] peds = pediatric medication dosage

Internet Resources

All sites were last accessed on January 10, 2003.
1. Centers for Disease Control: Home page
   www.cdc.gov
2. Centers for Disease Control: Bioterrorism page
   www.bt.cdc.gov
3. Centers for Disease Control: Health-Related Hoaxes and Rumors
   www.cdc.gov/hoax_rumors.htm
4. U.S. Army Medical Research and Materiel Command
   www.biomedtraining.org/
5. Textbook of Military Medicine, Medical Aspect of Chemical and Biological Warfare
   (download version)
   http://ccc.apgea.army.mil/reference_materials/textbook/
   HTML_Restricted/index_2.htm
6. The Terrorism Research Center
   www.terrorism.com/index.shtml
7. Association for Professionals in Infection Control and Epidemiology (APIC)
   www.apic.org/
8. National Terrorism Preparedness Institute
   http://terrorism.spjc.edu/
9. The Journal of Homeland Defense
   www.homelanddefense.org/journal/
10. NIH/Medline Plus Health Information: Biological and Chemical Weapons
    www.nlm.nih.gov/medlineplus/biologicalandchemicalweapons.html
11. HS/HSL Terrorism Resources for the Healthcare Community
    www.hshsl.umaryland.edu/resources/terrorism.html
12. btresponse.org: Resources for Medical Professionals
    www.btresponse.org/
13. ProMed-mail (the free subscription is highly recommended)
    www.promedmail.org
14. Food and Drug Administration (FDA): Bioterrorism page
    www.fda.gov/oc/opacom/hottopics/bioterrorism.html
15. USAMRIID's Medical Management of Biological Casualties Handbook
    (download version)
    www.usamriid.army.mil/education/bluebook.html

Biological and Chemical Terrorism
Quick Reference Telephone Numbers

Local Health Department

_____

Centers for Disease Control and Prevention (CDC)

404-639-2206 during business hours

404-639-2888 during other times

For our families, who tolerate knowing
much more about bioterrorism than
they would really care to know.

Acknowledgment

With many thanks to Michael Weinstein, John Symington, M.D., and Debra Scarborough, M.L.S., for their assistance in the preparation of this book.

Table of Contents

SECTION 3: INDIVIDUAL BIOLOGICAL WEAPON DETAILED QUICK REFERENCES

SECTION 4: BASIC CHEMICAL TERRORISM

SECTION 5: CHEMICAL WEAPON SYNDROMIC CROSS-REFERENCES

SECTION 6: INDIVIDUAL CHEMICAL WEAPON DETAILED QUICK REFERENCES

Foreword

Biological weapons pose serious and complex problems for the medical community and associated groups. The initial signs and symptoms of most infections caused by bioagents closely resemble those of early influenza in that they are mild and characterized on occasion by some fever, chest discomfort, headache, fatigue, and general malaise. This period of the incubation process represents the most opportune time for medical intervention. Notwithstanding, it would be difficult for most physicians to initiate serious therapy in light of these mild symptoms; yet, within hours, these symptoms become severe, and the infection becomes more difficult to treat and, in certain instances, leads to death. The deliberate release of an infectious, small-particle aerosol can drastically change incubation and pathogenesis of the "classic" disease reported in the medical literature. A case in point is the deliberate dissemination of a moderate grade of *Coxiella burnetii* slurry, the etiologic agent of Q fever. Mathematical modeling shows that the agent can cause an infection over 100 kilometers downwind of the release with 10 organisms and the classic incubation period of 10 to 17 days. At the point of dissemination, however, and 100 to 200 meters thereafter, the victim could receive a dose of more than 100,000 organisms. Under these circumstances, the incubation period is reduced to 5 days, and disease progression is significantly altered. Natural infections are simply not caused by such massive doses of agent.

The training and experience of Ken Alibek and Raymond Weinstein qualify them to address the recognition and management of biological casualties. The insightful information contained in this book will provide a comprehensive reference for biological warfare agents.

WILLIAM C. PATRICK III
President, Bio Threats Assessment
Former Chief of Product Development,
U.S. Biological Warfare Program

Preface

The purpose of this book is to provide medical professionals with a quickly accessible, useful, and accurate source of information to aid not only in the management of illnesses produced by biological and chemical weapons but also in the recognition that an attack with biological weapons has even taken place. Although recognizing an attack with biological weapons may sound as if it should be obvious, this is usually not the case in an unannounced attack. The realization may not actually take place until several days after the attack when many seriously ill patients begin showing up in emergency rooms and doctors' offices. The main thrust of this book will be to delineate biological weapons because they are so much more difficult to identify early in an attack than chemical weapons, and because the contagiousness of some could make an attack self-sustaining, rather than the single event seen in a chemical weapon attack. Chemical weapons are presented primarily because they are easily accessible, they are known to be in the hands of terrorist groups, and their effects can be devastating. Physicians must be prepared to deal with both kinds of terrorism.

Section 1, "Basic Bioterrorism," and Section 4, "Basic Chemical Terrorism," outline the basic principles of preparedness and defense for both types of attacks, while detailing the telltale signs of what might indicate the earliest evidence that such an attack has occurred. The charts in Section 2, "Biological Weapon Syndromic Cross-References," and Section 5, "Chemical Weapon Syndromic Cross-References," are designed to help lead the health care provider in the correct diagnostic direction, from symptoms to syndrome to specific disease, when confronted with a patient or cluster of patients with a suspicious presentation. Each page in the "Detailed Quick Reference" sections (Sections 3 and 6) is designed to be a complete and self-contained disease or weapon module for each of the most likely biological and chemical agents. They can be quickly referred to as an aid in confirming a suspected diagnosis and, in the event of a confirmed attack when the agent has already been identified, as a guide to the management of its victims. Some pages in this book are designed to be easily torn out or photocopied so they may be posted any place for quick reference in an emergency situation.

The list of weapons outlined in this book is by no means meant to be exhaustive and all-inclusive. There are literally hundreds of toxic chemicals in common use and many biological weapons, such as genetically altered or enhanced organisms, and bioregulator weapons, with which this book will not deal in detail.

Such biological weapons, with luck, would be beyond the financial and technical capacities of most, if not all, terrorist groups to obtain, maintain, or deploy. The weapons that are listed here are a combination of the most likely, the most easily obtainable, and potentially the most dangerous weapons to which a terrorist organization might gain access. Another agent that some consider a potential weapon, which is not covered in this book, is the epsilon toxin of *Clostridium perfringens*. Although the Centers for Disease

Control and Prevention presently lists it as a category B weapon and there has been the suggestion that Iraq has been trying to develop it as a weapon, in actuality, there has never been a human intoxication reported. This substance is highly toxic and often lethal to mice and certain ruminants, but at present its effect on humans remains uncertain. In susceptible animals, it is known to produce renal and cerebral edema following ingestion, and it produces a lethal pulmonary disease after inhalation by laboratory test animals.

It should be remembered that the diagnostic and treatment recommendations listed in this book are based on the currently accepted standards for diseases that, up to now, may have produced few recorded human cases. Should one of those biological weapons be used for a terrorist attack, it is likely that the recommendations for diagnosing and treating the illness it produces will evolve along with the evolution of the outbreak.

It is our hope that this book will help bridge the gap left by many other bioterrorism references that generally start off with the assumption that the healthcare provider should already know to which biological weapon his or her patients have fallen victim. Primary-care practitioners in their offices and emergency rooms will be the first line of defense in identifying an attack with biological weapons and may be called on to treat the victims of chemical weapons, and we must be ready. Short of actually preventing a terrorist attack with biological weapons, early detection of that attack and identification of the weapon used would be the most effective way to save lives.

RAYMOND WEINSTEIN
KEN ALIBEK

Introduction

Until recently, the threat of biological terrorism was pretty much theoretical, and the United States seemed almost immune to such an unthinkable attack. Certainly, there have been small, local, homegrown incidents, the most notable of which occurred in 1984 in the Oregon hamlet of The Dalles. As would be expected in a bioterrorism attack, the motive in The Dalles was political. A religious cult located in the community wanted to change the outcome of a municipal election, so 2 days before the polls opened members spread salmonella in several restaurant salad bars. The subsequent outbreak of 751 dysentery cases failed to change the outcome of the election, and in an unfortunate failure of the public health system, the entire event was merely chalked up to a widespread natural event. It was not until about a year later that a defector from the cult admitted to authorities that the outbreak had been an intentional attack. A subsequent investigation at the cult's compound revealed a crude laboratory with active cultures of *Salmonella typhimurium*, the organism that caused the outbreak.

On September 11, 2001, the secure complacency of the United States was shattered, and in the events that followed it became clear that America enjoys no special immunity from terrorism of any kind. Beginning on October 4, 2001, and continuing for several months, an outbreak of fatal inhalational anthrax gave everyone more to fear from their mail than just the monthly bills, and our sense of security evaporated in a puff of white powder. Eleven victims were infected with cutaneous anthrax and 11 with inhalational anthrax. Of the latter, five died of the illness and taught the medical community that we knew far less about anthrax than we had previously believed. The attack, which spread over six states and the District of Columbia, frightened a nation and paralyzed the mail in Washington, DC, and surrounding states, while disrupting the postal system throughout the entire county.

Imagine being a primary-care or emergency department physician in an area where anthrax had already been identified, knowing that the very next patient encountered could be the latest anthrax case. Now imagine the fear of being the physician to miss that diagnosis, allowing your patient to succumb to the deadly disease. The physicians in our community in northern Virginia did not have to imagine such a scenario; it was unexpectedly thrust on us. Only about 20 miles from Washington, DC, our community had three of the inhalational anthrax victims. Fortunately, all the patients were properly evaluated and managed, and all survived. Our success was due, in no small part, to preparation. We had formed a community-wide chemical and biological terrorism preparedness committee in 1999 and had actively sought to educate the medical community about biological and chemical terrorism while bringing together hospitals, physicians from hospitals and private practice, experts in the field of biological terrorism, and doctors and epidemiologists from the state health department. Dr. Raymond Weinstein, one of the editors of this book, is the organizer and chairman of that committee, and we cannot stress enough the importance of every hospital or community forming such a committee.

Because of our preparations, following the September 11 attacks, but before the first anthrax case ever appeared, we were able to distribute to physicians and emergency departments in our region, several one-page *Quick Reference* guides that could be displayed in prominent areas for use in quickly reviewing the presentation and initial management of several potential biological weapons. These *Quick References* were well received and have now achieved an international distribution via the Internet and postings to Web sites such as that of the Association for Professionals in Infection Control and Epidemiology (www.apic.org/). Because of their usefulness, we have prepared this comprehensive book of *Quick References* to aid doctors everywhere and to provide a bit more sense of security to those of us responsible for our patients' and our community's health and well-being.

> *Diagnosing an illness produced by a biological weapon is exactly the same as diagnosing any other flulike illness, pneumonia, rash, or acute gastroenteritis.*

There is little doubt that the future holds the strong possibility of further terrorist attacks with biological or chemical weapons against targets in the United States and in other countries. There are only two ways of mitigating a bioterrorism attack: by prevention, which is the domain of law enforcement, and by early detection with proper treatment, which falls to the medical community. Physicians in their offices and emergency rooms are our first and best line of defense. Making the correct diagnosis of a disease produced by a biological weapon is exactly the same as diagnosing any other illness. Practitioners within the medical community must be careful not to fall into the trap of fearing a disease merely because it fits into the biological weapons category. Most physicians already have the skills and experience to diagnose these diseases; they have only to consider them in the differential diagnosis. Of course, when in doubt, a call to the local health department can be very helpful in determining the proper next step in the evaluation and care of a suspected bioterrorism victim

How to Use This Book

This book is divided into six sections: (1) Basic Bioterrorism, (2) Biological Weapon Syndromic Cross-References, (3) Individual Biological Weapon Detailed Quick References, (4) Basic Chemical Terrorism, (5) Chemical Weapon Syndromic Cross-References, and (6) Individual Chemical Weapon Detailed Quick References. Section 1 describes how and when to suspect that an unusual disease outbreak is taking place and when to suspect that such an outbreak might be due to an attack with a biological weapon. Identifying an outbreak due to an attack is the first step in bioterrorism defense, and the reader should be familiar with this section prior to any suspicious disease outbreak. Section 4 provides similar information for chemical weapons, including how they are classified and disseminated, how they work, and what steps can be taken for personal protection not only from the agent itself but also from potentially contaminated patients.

Section 2 leads the reader through the identification of what would be the most likely biological weapon used in an early or ongoing attack. Nearly all the weapons have some presenting syndrome, or constellation of symptoms, in common with other weapons. For example, if a cluster of patients begins showing up with a flulike illness and a rash, or a fever with severe arthralgias, these syndromes can be found in this section. The page for the chosen syndrome contains a list of the most likely weapons along with a more complete description of their presenting symptoms. Each syndrome is listed with its page number.

From Section 2, the reader can choose the most likely individual weapon or weapons listed and find a detailed description of each in the third section of the book. In that section will be found a detailed description of the clinical presentation, clinical course, recommended methods of identification, recommended treatments, and personal precautions for each weapon.

Section 5 breaks down the presenting symptoms of the chemical weapons outlined in this book into the four syndromes listed. This section is less important for chemical weapons than for the corresponding section for biological weapons because the onset and presentation of symptoms linked to a chemical weapon attack are not as subtle or confusing as with biological weapons.

BASIC BIOTERRORISM

What Is Bioterrorism?

Bioterrorism can be defined as the intentional release, or threatened release, of disease-producing living organisms or biologically active substances derived from living organisms, for the purpose of causing death, illness, incapacity, economic damage, or fear. These organisms are considered weapons of mass destruction, or mass casualty weapons.

There are hundreds of potential biological weapons, including bacteria, viruses, genetically altered or enhanced infectious agents, vaccine and/or multidrug–resistant organisms, and toxins produced by organisms, some of which behave more like chemical than biological weapons. These weapons can be used for inciting panic and fear, paralyzing a nation, overwhelming medical services, causing severe economic damage, causing illness and death, and gaining a military advantage.

Many biological weapons are relatively inexpensive and easy to produce. Although the most sophisticated and effective versions require considerable equipment and specialized scientific expertise, primitive versions can be produced in a small, unobtrusive area, with minimal equipment and limited training. The former Soviet Union's Germ Warfare Program developed many such highly specialized biological weapons. One such weapon consists of a *Yersinia pseudotuberculosis* bacterium that produces an initial, seemingly ordinary febrile illness, followed shortly by a severe progressive demyelinating neuropathy that leaves its victims completely paralyzed. Other unusual and dangerous weapons developed by the Russian program include hybrid (chimera) viruses that might simultaneously produce both smallpox and Ebola; bacterial proviruses that produce an initial case of plague, then release Venezuelan equine encephalitis virus when exposed to antibiotics; a prion weapon that produces a mad cow disease–like illness; stealth viruses that lay dormant within the victim until activated at a later time; and the previously mentioned bioregulator weapons.

Bioregulator weapons provoke the production of excessive amounts of normally occurring biological substances, producing a hugely exaggerated and detrimental physiologic response. Such weapons presently known to exist include a bacterium that produces large quantities of endorphins, which can cause extreme lethargy or even catatonia in addition to whatever usual pathological effects that organism produces, and an organism that produces excessive neurokinin P (substance P), which can cause sudden vasodilation with severe hypotension or shock, and bronchoconstriction with severe shortness of breath.

The Soviet biological weapons research program lasted for over 50 years, until its official dissolution by Boris Yeltsin in 1992. In that time, the Soviet program not only caught up with the U.S. program, behind which it had lagged by about 5 years, but it became, by far, the most sophisticated biological weapons program in the world. The present status of these weapons in the former Soviet arsenal is not entirely known.

The use of biological weapons in wartime is not a new concept. The first recorded instances date back to the sixth century B.C., when the Assyrians poisoned enemy wells with rye ergot to disable them with ergotism, or St. Anthony's fire, as it was known in the Middle Ages. At about the same time, the Greeks were employing the purgative herb hellebore to "occupy" their enemies during the siege of Krissa. Many such instances involving the military use of living organisms or toxins exist throughout history.

In the twentieth century, the development of biological weapons reached a fever pitch with well-organized and well-funded biological warfare programs in Germany and Japan during World War II, and in the United States and the Soviet Union during the cold war. The United States dismantled its biowarfare program in the 1960s, but the Russians, who at the time denied having such a program, produced tons of traditional disease weapons and many innovative and extremely dangerous new weapons. After the breakup of the Soviet Union and the subsequent prolonged economic crisis that occurred there, many of the scientists who helped develop and refine the Russian biological weapons found themselves without jobs or, if still employed, without paychecks. A number of them left Russia and found their way to oil-rich third world countries, such as Iraq, which actively support terrorism, and where their knowledge and skills were highly prized. Some of the scientists are believed to have left Russia with samples and seed cultures in their pockets with which they could easily begin developing new biological weapons programs. From these countries, some of the most dangerous weapons are known to have found their way into the hands of international terrorist organizations that undoubtedly would use them against their perceived enemies at the first opportunity.

Although this book deals only with human diseases, it is important to remember that not all biological weapons directly target human beings. There is a great potential for disrupting food supplies and producing huge economic damage with weapons aimed at farm animals and crops. Foot and mouth disease would be just such a potential weapon even though it does not produce any significant human illness.

Categorizing Biological Weapons

The Centers for Disease Control and Prevention (CDC) prioritizes biological weapons as categories A, B, and C, according to such qualities as their accessibility, ease of use, potential for social disruption, morbidity, mortality, and contagiousness.

CATEGORY A
- Can be easily disseminated and/or transmitted from person to person
- Cause high mortality and have the potential for major public health impact
- Might cause public panic and social disruption
- Require special action for public health preparedness

Included in this category are such diseases as plague, smallpox, viral hemorrhagic fevers, botulism, tularemia, and anthrax.

CATEGORY B
- Are moderately easy to disseminate
- Cause moderate morbidity and low mortality
- Require specific enhancements of the CDC's diagnostic capacity and enhanced disease surveillance

This category includes the toxins or agents of diseases such as brucellosis, glanders, Q fever, ricin, abrin, trichothecene (T-2) mycotoxins, and staphylococcus enterotoxin B.

CATEGORY C
- These third highest priority agents include emerging pathogens that could be engineered for mass dissemination in the future because of
  - availability,
  - ease of production and dissemination, and
  - potential for high morbidity and mortality and major health impact.

This category includes diseases such as the Hantaviruses, multidrug-resistant tuberculosis, tick-borne encephalitis and hemorrhagic fever viruses, and yellow fever.

Agents may also be separated into groups according to type, such as bacteria, virus, fungus, or toxin. The illnesses they produce can be divided according to their most prominent symptoms or the syndromes they produce, such as pneumonia or acute respiratory distress with and without fever, flulike illness with rash, neurologic syndromes with and without fever, and acute gastrointestinal (GI) syndromes with and without fever. A more complete listing of such syndromes can be found in Section 2 of this book. However they are classified or categorized, the most important factor is to consider them when confronted with an ill patient, especially if an attack with one or more biological weapons has already been announced or identified.

Flulike Illness

Many biological weapons have an initial presentation similar to that of influenza. This presentation has come to be known as a flulike illness (FLI) or influenza-like illness (ILI). The CDC lists the symptoms of influenza as the rapid onset of fever, malaise or fatigue, myalgias, headache, cough, sore throat, and nasal congestion. Any syndrome that presents with most or all of these symptoms fits the category of flulike illness. A large number of currently recognized biological weapons present in just that way and must be differentiated from common influenza as quickly as possible. One way to make this differentiation is to look at some of the other symptoms associated with these biological weapons, such as chest pain, rash, hemoptysis, and prominent gastrointestinal symptoms, which are not common with influenza. Additionally, sore throat and nasal congestion are common presenting symptoms of influenza, but sore throat occurs in only a handful of biological weapons, and nasal congestion is common only after exposure to trichothecene mycotoxins. A comparison of influenza to the presenting symptoms of most of the likely biological weapons can be found in Table 1.

What Makes an Effective Weapon?

There are a number of qualities and factors that make a particular agent appealing to a terrorist (or the military) for use as a biological weapon. The type of attack planned, the resources of the terrorist or group, and the goals of the attack (i.e., kill, incapacitate, frighten, or disrupt) will dictate the weapon of choice.

INEXPENSIVE AND EASY TO PRODUCE

Anthrax is a good example of a weapon that can be acquired or produced in large quantities for under $100. It can be found in soil in most parts of the world and is easily and rapidly grown in culture with minimal equipment and little expertise. Even though smallpox would make a much more devastating weapon, it would be extremely expensive or even impossible to acquire for the majority of terrorist organizations, and it requires expensive equipment and special skills to adequately maintain it.

EASY TO WEAPONIZE

Depending on the delivery system employed, the physical characteristics of the weapon become very important. There are several potential methods for releasing a biological weapon that include dispersal into the air as an aerosol, mist, or powder, contamination of food or water, topical exposure with absorption through the skin, and release of an infected insect vector. This is the area where anthrax loses some of its appeal. The most effective way to release anthrax and infect a large number of victims is by dispersal of an aerosol or powder, but for this to be effective, the spore particles must be between 1 and 6 microns in size. If they are larger, they will only lodge in the upper airways; if they are too small, they will just be exhaled with the next breath. It is difficult and expensive to produce an anthrax aerosol that is consistently the correct size. What made the anthrax used in the October 2001 mailings so deadly was that nearly all the particles were milled to the correct size and it was manufactured in such a way as to prevent clumping due to the electrostatic charge of the particles. It was a very sophisticated weapon, and undoubtedly was extremely expensive and difficult to produce.

EASY TO DISSEMINATE

Obviously, any weapon that requires little or no skill to disseminate would be preferred. Releasing a fine powder or aerosol in a crowded public place or into the breeze off a high building is generally accepted as the scenario most likely to occur because it is the simplest. The Hollywood movie scenario of the furtive midnight addition of a vial of toxic agent into a large water supply, like a reservoir, is very unlikely because no agent could escape the problems of massive dilution and subsequent water processing. It would literally require a tanker truck full of agent to successfully infect or poison a large water supply.

EASY TO HIDE AND TRANSPORT

In most cases, a biological weapon will have to be smuggled into the country from abroad. A weapon that requires large quantities to be effective or has special storage requirements such as extreme cold would be much more difficult to hide or might not survive a prolonged trip. Production of the weapon within the borders of the target country would alleviate this problem.

SHORT AND PREDICTABLE INCUBATION PERIOD

This would allow the terrorists time to escape before their act was uncovered while occurring soon enough to allow for rapid gratification and political exploitation. One of the factors that differentiates biological from chemical terrorism is the delay in the onset of symptoms for most biological weapons. In chemical terrorism, the victims literally drop like flies, whereas an attack with a biological weapon will usually have an insidious onset, with increasing numbers of victims becoming sick over several days. One reason why the human immunodeficiency virus (HIV) would make such a poor weapon is that terrorists would have to wait so many years to realize and exploit the results of their act.

MAINTAINS POTENCY AND PERSISTS IN THE ENVIRONMENT

Many of the bacterial and viral weapons are highly sensitive to ultraviolet (UV) light, heat, cold, and dessication. There is sufficient ambient UV light, even at sunset, to quickly kill many of these organisms. A good example of this is rabies. The Russians attempted to create a rabies bioweapon, but great difficulties of production and a very short survival

TABLE 1 Comparison of Initial Symptoms of Potential Biological Weapons to Influenza (Flulike Illness)

	Rapid Onset	Fever	Chills	Malaise or Fatigue	Myalgias	Headache	Sore Throat	Cough	Nasal Congestion	GI[1] Symptoms	Joint or Back Pain	Chest Tightness	Pleuritic Chest Pain	Dyspnea	Hemoptysis	Rash
Influenza[2]	X	X	X	X	X	X	X	X	X	Rare						
Anthrax (inhalational)	X	X	X	X	X	X	Rare	X	Rare	X		X		X		
Blastomycosis		X	X	X	X			X			X		X	X	X	
Brucellosis (acute)	X	X	X	X	X	X		X		X	X		X	X		
Cholera		X				X				X						
Crimean Congo & Rift Valley fevers	X	X		X							X					
Dengue fever	X	X	X	X	X	X				X	X					X
Glanders	X	X	X		X	X				X			X			X
Hantavirus pulmonary syndrome	X	X	X	X		X		X		X				X		
Lassa virus & hemorrhagic fevers[2]		X		X	X	X	X	X		X	X	X				
Legionnaires' disease	X	X	X	X	X	X		X		X		X			X	
Leptospirosis	X	X	X	X	X	X	X			X	X					X
Marburg & Ebola virus[2]	X	X	X	X	X	X	X	X		X						X

Melioidosis[2]	X	X	X	X	X	X								
Nipah virus[2]	X	X	X	X	X	X								
Plague[2]	X	X	X	X	X	X	X				X		X	
Psittacosis[2]	X	X	X	X	X	<50%	X	<50%	X	X	Rare	<50%	Rare	Rare
Q fever	X	X	X	X	X	25%		25%	X	X	X	25%		
Ricin & abrin	X	X				X	X	X	X			X		
RMSF[3]	X	X	X	X	X	X	X	X	X					X
Smallpox[2]	X	X	X	X	X	X	X	X	X					X
Staphylococcal enterotoxin B (inhalation)	X	X	X		X	X	X	X	X		X			
Trichothecene mycotoxins	X	X	X	X	X	X	X	X	X	X	X			
Tularemia (pulmonary)	X	X	X	X	X	X	X	X			X	X		
Typhoid fever	X	X	X	X	X	X	X	X	X					
Typhus	X	X	X	X	X	X	X	X	X				X	
Venezuelan equine (viral) encephalitis	X	X	X	X	X	X	X	X	X	X				

[1] Nausea, vomiting, diarrhea, hematochezia, and/or abdominal pain
[2] Contagious via direct person-to-person contact
[3] Rocky Mountain spotted fever
GI = gastrointestinal

TABLE 2   **Common Biological Weapons and Their Survival Time in the Environment after Release**

Weapon	Survival Time
Anthrax	Days to weeks in the air, years on surfaces
Brucellosis	Up to 2 days in the air
Coccidioidomycosis	Days to weeks in the air
Glanders	Several hours in the air
Marburg virus	30 min liquid form and hours in dry form, in the air
Plague	One to 2 hr in the air
Q fever	Up to several days in the air
Smallpox	Up to 24 hr in the air, up to 1 month on surfaces
Tularemia	Up to 24 hr in the air

time after release, consisting of only minutes, made it an unacceptable weapon. Some other survival times are listed in Table 2.

ILLNESS PRODUCED IS LETHAL AND/OR INCAPACITATING

The goals of bioterrorism are usually not just to kill, but also to disrupt the target society and to induce fear and panic in its population. Producing an illness that leaves hundreds or thousands of victims incapacitated yet medically salvageable would completely overwhelm the medical infrastructure. For example, no medical system could accommodate 500 patients suddenly presenting with severe pneumonia or acute paralysis and all requiring mechanical ventilation. No facility or even multifacility hospital system would have that many ventilators on hand. The chaos that might follow so many family members watching their loved ones die from what they perceive as a lack of medical attention would be devastating, not to mention the huge demoralizing effect it would have on the already overburdened and disheartened healthcare providers trying to deal with the situation.

One way to mitigate such a situation is by forethought and preparation. Every hospital or community should have biological and chemical terrorism response plans already in place. A standing committee dedicated to such preparations is presently the most effective way to plan and prepare a response. For example, such a committee would know that in the United States, the National Pharmaceutical Stockpile could be expected to arrive within 12 hours of being activated by the CDC or the Federal Emergency Management Agency (FEMA). It would include over 50 tons of medical supplies, from medications to surgical supplies to mechanical ventilators.

Every healthcare provider and first responder should have a working knowledge of potential biological weapons and the special problems created by the mass casualties they would produce. Medical responses should be practiced from time to time as part of the hospital or community disaster plan. This would allow for the identification of weaknesses and needs and aid in the prior identification of available resources, even at some distance away. These preparations alone would go a long way toward lessening the effectiveness of any biological weapon that might be used.

ILLNESS PRODUCED IS DIFFICULT OR IMPOSSIBLE TO TREAT

Several of the viruses and toxins have no specific treatment, although most can be successfully managed through supportive care alone, and some, such as smallpox, anthrax, and yellow fever, can be prevented by early vaccination. For the purposes of bioterrorism, the use of a disease that has no specific treatment would provide an additional psychological advantage.

ILLNESS PRODUCED IS HIGHLY CONTAGIOUS

Only a handful of the weapons outlined in this book have the potential for direct person-to-person transmission through aerosols or droplets. Some of those weapons include smallpox, Nipah virus, Ebola and the other hemorrhagic fever viruses, plague, psittacosis, and melioidosis. The advantages of a contagious weapon are obvious, because secondary cases would affect a greater number of victims and put an additional burden on the medical infrastructure.

NAME OF THE DISEASE INDUCES FEAR

This may not seem like a very important point, but from a psychological point of view, it can be. As was so memorably illustrated in the movie *Jaws*, no one ever flees the water when someone shouts "Barracuda!" but yell "Shark!" and you have a panic on your hands. This mentality also holds true for biological weapons. If the general population hears on the news that there has been a number of unexplained cases of melioidosis, Marburg virus, or leptospirosis, many will remain unconcerned. But if it is announced that there is an unexplained outbreak of anthrax, plague, Ebola, or smallpox, there will very likely be a panicked dash for the nearest doctor's office or emergency room, as well as a run on antibiotics. This is exactly what occurred after the anthrax letters of 2001, and that panic was in response to only 11 cases spread out from Florida to Connecticut.

Early Identification of a Bioterrorist Attack

The importance of early identification of an attack with a biological weapon cannot be overstated. It is paramount for saving lives. There are two types of attacks to consider, announced and unannounced. In an announced attack, the perpetrator publicly discloses the details of the attack in order to produce widespread fear. In such an attack, the weapon employed would probably be known even before the first victims began developing symptoms, allowing for preparation and the institution of preventive measures by the medical and public health communities. An unannounced attack would be much more dangerous and insidious. Healthcare providers would have no warning, and would not even realize an attack had taken place until many previously well patients with similar symptoms began clamoring for medical care. In such an attack, it is likely that the first patients to become ill would die because the etiology of their illness would be attributed to a common pathogen like influenza, until it was too late. This exact scenario occurred in the October 2001 anthrax attacks.

Another important consideration is the fact that terrorists are not confined to the use of a single agent. The simultaneous release of more than one biological weapon might result in confusing clusters of patients with similar but slightly different illnesses, such as plague and tularemia, which both produce an initial flulike illness with a gram-negative pneumonia, or they might produce widely divergent symptoms such as those seen in the simultaneous release of plague and botulinum toxin.

Once an unannounced attack has been identified, physicians can be alerted to watch for the appropriate symptoms, and hospitals can stockpile the appropriate remedies.

Undoubtedly, in the event of such an attack, it will be an astute physician in an office or emergency room who will be the first to make the diagnosis, or realize that there have been just too many unexplainable pneumonias or unusual rashes in the last 3 or 4 days. It might even be a first responder who notices a sudden increase of ambulance runs for seriously ill patients or a pharmacist who notes a sudden rise in requests for over-the-counter flu or cough medications. Whomever that person is, he or she would then alert the local public health authorities, and a general announcement could be made to warn everyone. The actions of that one astute individual would save countless lives.

There are two types of disease surveillance that can help uncover a bioterrorist attack, syndromic and epidemiologic. Syndromic surveillance is what many public health departments do when they track the daily number of influenza cases throughout the year. It allows them to uncover a sudden increase from the baseline. Should this occur at an unexpected time or within a very limited location, it can trigger a closer investigation. This kind of organized and labor-intensive surveillance is not appropriate for most practicing healthcare providers.

Epidemiologic surveillance is what every physician does automatically when noticing an unexpected change in the frequency or type of illnesses being seen. There are actually several categories of suspicious changes about which health care providers should be aware (see Table 3). These lists are not meant to be all-inclusive but to suggest the kinds of occurrences that should raise a suspicion in an astute clinician and provoke a call to the local health department.

Personal Precautions

The majority of biological weapons are not easily transmitted person–to–person. Although blood, urine, or tissue specimens may be infectious, it is usually not possible to catch a disease produced by biological weapons by merely being in the same examining room with or touching an infected patient. In fact, the examining physician is less likely to catch a disease produced by a biological weapon, from a patient, than he or she is to catch a cold or pharyngitis. In most cases, no special precautions or equipment are required except the standard precautions that should be part of every practice. Some exceptions to this are smallpox, the hemorrhagic fevers, plague, Nipah virus, and possibly melioidosis, which all require special precautions. The precautions for each potential weapon can be found listed in Section 3 of this book. Secondary cases of most of these can be prevented by immunization, prophylactic antibiotics, and proper infection control techniques.

Both Sections 2 and 3 contain information about what precautions should be followed for each specific biological weapon.

Accepted patient isolation precautions are as follows:
- **Standard precautions:** Wash hands after patient contact, and wear gloves whenever there is risk of contact with blood, secretions, body fluids, or contaminated items. Wear a mask, gown, and eye protection when there is a risk of splashing contaminated fluids. Clean stethoscopes and other equipment with alcohol after examining a potentially infectious or contaminated patient.
- **Airborne precautions:** This includes standard precautions, plus putting the patient or cohorting patients in a negative air pressure room for the purpose of preventing the inhalation of droplet nuclei less than 6 microns and/or contaminated dusk particles by the uninfected. Wear respiratory protection when entering the room consisting of a

TABLE 3 **Signs That Suggest an Attack with a Biological Weapon**

- **Illnesses out of range:**
  - a sudden, unexplained increase in the number of flulike illnesses over a short period of time, especially in a young and healthy population
  - a high percentage of patients with flulike symptoms with a negative rapid influenza test or culture
  - a sudden unexplained cluster of patients with rash, pneumonia, hemorrhagic symptoms, death, or requiring hospital (especially ICU) admission
  - any sudden increase in morbidity or mortality associated with a seemingly common illness, such as influenza or chickenpox
  - a sudden and unexpected increase in the number of patient phone calls for influenza, rash, neurologic symptoms, lower respiratory symptoms, or requests for antibiotics
- **Illnesses out of context:**
  - an outbreak of flulike illness in a well-immunized population
  - neurological or stroke symptoms in young and previously healthy patients
  - an outbreak of chickenpox-like rash in a varicella immune population
  - flulike illness associated with unusual complications such as hemorrhage, hepatitis, pneumonia, acute respiratory distress syndrome, lymphadenopathy, or rash
  - a cluster of treatment failures in an illness that usually responds to, or would be expected to respond to the utilized therapy
- **Illnesses out of sequence:**
  - an outbreak of illness affecting only one age group, sex, ethnic group, or only those who work in a particular facility
  - clusters of human illness simultaneous to, or immediately following, reports of an outbreak of animal disease or death in the same geographic region
  - a human outbreak of any equine encephalitis with no reports of preceding equine cases
- **Illnesses out of season:**
  - an influenza outbreak in the late spring or summer
  - an outbreak of an illness that is typically arthropod borne occurring in winter when arthropods would be dormant (e.g., Rocky Mountain spotted fever, tick- or mosquito-borne encephalitis, plague, and typhus)
- **Illness out of place:**
  - the occurrence of even one case of a potential biological weapon in a location where it would not be expected to naturally occur. An exception would be in any patient who has returned from an endemic area for that illness and the onset of symptoms occurred within the expected incubation period. Examples would be the occurrence of even one case of Ebola, smallpox, Nipah, Omsk hemorrhagic fever, or Kyasanur Forest disease in the United States or Great Britain.
- **What to do when you become suspicious of an unusual disease outbreak or clusters of patients with unusual symptoms:**
  - Call your local health department and let officials know.
  - If you do not have a local health department, call your state or regional health department, or the Centers for Disease Control and Prevention in Atlanta.
  - Write the phone number of your local, regional, or state health department here:

Modified with permission from Jonathan Temte, M.D.

HEPA (N-95 or better) filter mask, and place a mask on the patient if transport to another area is required.

- **Droplet precautions:** This includes standard precautions, plus placing the patient or cohorting patients in a private room. Wear at least a surgical mask when working within 3 feet of an infected patient, and place a mask on the patient if transport to another area is required.

- **Contact precautions:** This includes standard precautions, plus placing the patient or cohorting patients in a private room. Wear a gown and gloves when entering the room, and change them after contact with infected material. Dedicate noncritical patient care equipment such as stethoscopes to a single patient or cohort. If this is not feasible, clean and disinfect such equipment after contact with the patient(s).

By following these simple precautions, physicians, nurse practitioners, nurses, and first responders will protect themselves, their coworkers, and their families from possible exposure to a dangerous disease.

The isolation precautions recommended in this book for several of the viral hemorrhagic fevers (Ebola, Marburg, Lassa, and Crimean-Congo hemorrhagic fevers, Omsk, South American, and Rift Valley fever, and Kyasanur Forest disease) do not conform to traditionally accepted precautions for these diseases and are based on the consensus statement published in the *Journal of the American Medical Association* on May 8, 2002.[22] The additional precautions are suggested until the risk of person-to-person airborne transmission of these viruses can be further investigated.

BIOLOGICAL WEAPON

SYNDROMIC CROSS-REFERENCES

Fever with Prominent Arthralgias

Disease/Agent	Incubation	Initial Symptoms
Blastomycosis (*Blastomyces dermatitidis*) see page 42	30–45 days	Sudden onset of fever, chills, myalgia, arthralgia, cough, and fatigue. 60% develop productive cough, hemoptysis, pleuritic chest pain, low-grade fever, dyspnea, and chest x-ray findings of infiltrates, nodules and/or cavitations. Hilar adenopathy may also be present.
Brucellosis (*Brucella suis & melitensis*) see page 46	Days to months	Intermittent fever, chills, sweats, headache, myalgia, arthralgias, back pain, generalized weakness, malaise, anorexia, nausea, vomiting, diarrhea and/or constipation. Cough and pleuritic chest pain in up to 20% of patients. Chest x-ray is variable and may show hilar adenopathy, pleural effusion nodules, abscesses, and/or bronchopneumonia.
Chikungunya (*Alphavirus*) see page 48	1–12 days	Abrupt onset of high fever, chills, severe headache, retro-orbital pain, flushing of face and trunk followed by a maculopapular rash of trunk and extremities, and migratory small joint arthralgias (hands, wrists, ankles, & feet primarily) which may be severe. A dengue hemorrhagic fever–like syndrome may occur rarely, especially in children.
Coccidioidomycosis (*Coccidioides immitis*) see page 52	7–21 days	Fever, dry cough, dyspnea, chest pain, and fatigue. Weight loss, migratory arthralgias, and headache are also common. Chest x-ray often demonstrates unilateral infiltrates, effusions, and hilar adenopathy. Pulmonary nodules and cavitations may also be seen occasionally. Rash is common, with early fine papular, nonpruritic rash that progressing to erythema nodosum and/or erythema multiforme (consider this diagnosis in the triad of fever, erythema nodosum, and arthralgias). May progress to superficial maculopapular lesions, cutaneous ulcers, subcutaneous abscesses, and/or lymphadenopathy.
Dengue fever and **dengue hemorrhagic fever (DHF)** (*Flavivirus*) see page 56	3–7 days	Sudden onset of fever, chills, malaise, arthralgias, myalgias, severe frontal headache, flushing, prominent low back pain, and dysesthesia of the skin. May also include prostration, gastrointestinal symptoms, hepatitis, macular or scarlatiniform rash, petechiae, and mucosal bleeding. May progress to DHF with hypotension, restlessness, diaphoresis, diffuse petechiae and ecchymosis, mucosal and gastrointestinal bleeding, ascites, organomegaly, cyanosis, and sudden shock.
Kyasanur Forest disease (*Flavivirus*) see page 68	2–9 days	Sudden onset of fever, chills, headache, vomiting, severe prostration, pains in arms and legs, flushing of face (no rash), conjunctival suffusion, hepatosplenomegaly, petechiae, general lymphadenopathy, and relative bradycardia. 40% of cases will develop gastrointestinal and mucosal bleeding, and/or hemorrhagic pulmonary edema. 50% of patients develop neurologic sequelae following 1–3 week afebrile period.
Omsk hemorrhagic fever (*Flavivirus*) see page 79	2–9 days	Sudden onset of fever, chills, headache, arthralgias, severe prostration, pains in arms and legs, flushing of face and trunk (no rash), conjunctival suffusion, papulovesicular eruption on soft palate, cervical lymphadenopathy, and relative bradycardia. GI and mucosal bleeding, and petechiae may occur. Neurologic sequelae or rarely pneumonia may occur late.

*Remittent fevers** are those that go up and down without ever returning to normal, as opposed to **intermittent fevers,** which are elevated with irregular returns to normal, and **relapsing fevers,** which are elevated with regular returns to normal.

Acute Hepatic Syndrome

Disease/Agent	Incubation	Initial Symptoms
Aflatoxins (*Aspergillus* species) see page 36	Days to weeks	Acute hepatic necrosis with fever, jaundice, edema of the limbs, abdominal pain, nausea, vomiting, pulmonary edema, GI hemorrhaging, hepatomegaly, seizures, coma, and death.
Crimean-Congo hemorrhagic fever (*Bunyaviridae*) see page 54	7–12 days	Sudden onset of fever, malaise, generalized weakness, back pain, and asthenia. May progress to fulminant disease with hepatitis, jaundice, DIC, shock, extensive bleeding, and death.
Ebola & Marburg viral hemorrhagic fevers (*Filoviridae*) see page 59	3–14 days	Sudden onset of fever, chills, headache, myalgia, generalized weakness, prostration, cough, sore throat, and conjunctivitis. May progress to nausea, vomiting, diarrhea, abdominal pain, photophobia, maculopapular rash, DIC, internal and external hemorrhages, multiorgan failure with jaundice and renal insufficiency, death.
Dengue fever and **Dengue hemorrhagic fever (DHF)** (*Flavivirus*) see page 56	3–7 days	Sudden onset of fever, chills, malaise, myalgias, severe frontal headache, flushing, prominent low back pain, and dysesthesia of the skin. May also include prostration, GI symptoms, hepatitis, macular or scarlatiniform rash, petechiae, and mucosal bleeding. May progress to DHF with hypotension, restlessness, diaphoresis, diffuse petechiae and ecchymosis, mucosal and GI bleeding, ascites, organomegaly, cyanosis, and sudden shock.
Leptospirosis (*Leptospira* species) see page 74	3–30 days	Sudden onset of remittent fever,* chills or rigors, headache, myalgia, low back pain, and conjunctival injection. May also include cough, abdominal pain, nausea, vomiting, diarrhea, sore throat, and/or a pretibial maculopapular rash. May progress to high fever, hepatitis, jaundice, liver failure, acute renal failure, hemorrhagic pneumonitis with hemoptysis, ARDS, bleeding diathesis, cardiac arrhythmias, shock, and death.
Q fever (*Coxiella burnetii*) see page 84	2–14 days	High fever, chills, malaise, fatigue, headache, anorexia, and myalgias. May progress to atypical pneumonia or hepatitis.
Ricin (castor bean extract) & **abrin** (rosary pea extract) see page 86	4–8 hr	Abdominal pain, nausea, vomiting, gastrointestinal hemorrhage with hematemesis and hematochezia. May progress to necrosis of the liver, spleen and/or kidneys, and shock.
Rift Valley fever (*Bunyaviridae*) see page 88	7–12 days	Sudden onset of fever, malaise, generalized weakness, back pain, and asthenia. May progress to fulminant disease with hepatitis, jaundice, DIC, shock, extensive bleeding, and death. Blindness and/or a fatal encephalitis may occur rarely.

*Remittent fevers** are those that go up and down without ever returning to normal, as opposed to **intermittent fevers,** which are elevated with irregular returns to normal, and **relapsing fevers,** which are elevated with regular returns to normal.

ARDS = acute respiratory distress syndrome; DIC = disseminated intravascular coagulation; GI = gastrointestinal

Hemorrhagic Diathesis

Disease/Agent	Incubation	Initial Symptoms
Aflatoxins (*Aspergillus* species) see page 36	Days to weeks	Acute hepatic necrosis with fever, jaundice, edema of the limbs, abdominal pain, nausea, vomiting, pulmonary edema, GI hemorrhaging, hepatomegaly, seizures, coma, and death.
Crimean-Congo hemorrhagic fever (*Bunyaviridae*) see page 54	7–12 days	Sudden onset of fever, malaise, generalized weakness, back pain, and asthenia. May progress to fulminant disease with hepatitis, jaundice, DIC, shock, extensive bleeding, and death.
Chikungunya (*Alphavirus*) see page 48	1–12 days	Abrupt onset of high fever, chills, severe headache, retro-orbital pain, flushing of face and trunk followed by a maculopapular rash of trunk and extremities, and migratory small joint arthralgias (hands, wrists, ankles & feet primarily), which may be severe. A dengue hemorrhagic fever-like syndrome may occur rarely, especially in children.
Dengue fever and **dengue hemorrhagic fever (DHF)** (*Flavivirus*) see page 56	3–7 days	Sudden onset of fever, chills, malaise, arthralgias, myalgias, severe frontal headache, flushing, prominent low back pain, and dysthesia of the skin. May also include prostration, GI symptoms, hepatitis, macular or scarlatiniform rash, petechiae, and mucosal bleeding. May progress to DHF with hypotension, restlessness, diaphoresis, diffuse petechiae and ecchymosis, mucosal and GI bleeding, ascites, organomegaly, cyanosis, and sudden shock.
Ebola & Marburg viral hemorrhagic fevers (*Filoviridae*) see page 59	3–14 days	Sudden onset of fever, chills, headache, myalgia, generalized weakness, prostration, cough, sore throat, and conjunctivitis. May progress to nausea, vomiting, diarrhea, abdominal pain, photophobia, maculopapular rash, DIC, internal and external hemorrhages, and multiorgan failure.
Hantavirus hemorrhagic fever with renal syndrome see page 64	5–24 days	Sudden onset of fever, chills, myalgias, headache, dizziness, low back pain, abdominal pain, conjunctival injection, blurred vision, erythematous rash on trunk and face, petechiae over upper trunk and on soft palate, and sudden severe shock and death. Survivors develop 3–10 days of mucosal bleeding, oliguria or anuria, hypertension, pneumonitis, and/or pulmonary edema.
Kyasanur Forest disease (*Flavivirus*) see page 68	2–9 days	Sudden onset of fever, chills, headache, vomiting, severe prostration, pains in arms and legs, flushing of face (no rash), conjunctival suffusion, hepatosplenomegaly, petechiae, general lymphadenopathy and relative bradycardia. 40% of cases will develop GI and mucosal bleeding and/or hemorrhagic pulmonary edema. 50% of patients develop neurologic sequelae following 1–3 week afebrile period.
Lassa virus & the South American viral hemorrhagic fevers (*Arenaviruses*) see page 70	3–19 days	Fever, malaise, myalgia, dysesthesia, abdominal pain, chest pain, back pain, sore throat, headache, vomiting, cough, photophobia, conjunctival injection, and flushing of face and upper trunk. May progress to hypotension, facial edema, pulmonary edema, vesicular and/or petechiae rash of oropharynx, mucosal hemorrhages, and occasionally pleural effusion, ascites.
Leptospirosis (*Leptospira* species) see page 74	3–30 days	Sudden onset of remittent fever,* chills or rigors, headache, myalgia, low back pain, and conjunctival injection. May also include cough, abdominal pain, nausea, vomiting, diarrhea, pharyngitis, and/or a pretibial maculopapular rash. May progress to high fever, liver failure, acute renal failure, aseptic meningitis, hemorrhagic pneumonitis with hemoptysis, ARDS, bleeding diathesis, cardiac arrhythmias, shock, and death.

Hemorrhagic Diathesis

Omsk hemorrhagic fever (Flavivirus) see page 79	2–9 days	Sudden onset of fever,* chills, headache, severe prostration, pains in arms and legs, flushing of face and trunk (no rash), conjunctival suffusion, papulovesicular eruption on soft palate, cervical lymphadenopathy, and relative bradycardia. GI and mucosal bleeding, and petechiae may occur. Neurologic sequelae or rarely pneumonia may occur late.
Ricin (castor bean extract) & **abrin** (rosary pea extract) see page 86	4–8 hr	Abdominal pain, nausea, vomiting, gastrointestinal hemorrhage with hematemesis and hematochezia. May progress to necrosis of the liver, spleen, and/or kidneys, and shock.
Rift Valley fever (*Bunyaviridae*) see page 88	7–12 days	Sudden onset of fever, malaise, generalized weakness, back pain, and asthenia. May progress to fulminant disease with hepatitis, jaundice, DIC, shock, extensive bleeding, and death. Blindness and/or a fatal encephalitis may occur rarely.

*Remittent fevers** are those that go up and down without ever returning to normal, as opposed to **intermittent fevers,** which are elevated with irregular returns to normal, and **relapsing fevers,** which are elevated with regular returns to normal.
ARDS = acute respiratory distress syndrome; DIC = disseminated intravascular coagulation; GI = gastrointestinal

Hilar Adenopathy or Widened Mediastinum

Disease/Agent	Incubation	Initial Symptoms
Anthrax, inhalational (*Bacillus anthracis*) see page 38	1–6 days	24–48 hr of fever (or recent history of fever), chills, cough, malaise, headache, myalgias, and possible chest tightness. Malaise may be profound and notable. Mediastinal widening or hilar adenopathy, and/or pleural effusion on CXR. Progresses to high fever, extreme fatigue, nonproductive cough, dyspnea, severe respiratory distress, cyanosis, septicemia, and death.
Blastomycosis (*Blastomyces dermatitidis*) see page 42	30–45 days	Sudden onset of fever, chills, myalgia, arthralgia, cough, and fatigue. 60% develop productive cough, hemoptysis, pleuritic chest pain, low-grade fever, dyspnea, and CXR findings of infiltrates, nodules, and/or cavitations. Hilar adenopathy may also be present.
Brucellosis (*Brucella suis & melitensis*) see page 46	Days to months	Intermittent fever, chills, sweats, headache, myalgia, arthralgias, back pain, generalized weakness, malaise, anorexia, nausea, vomiting, diarrhea and/or constipation. Cough and pleuritic chest pain in up to 20% of patients. CXR is variable and may show hilar adenopathy, pleural effusion nodules, abscesses, and/or bronchopneumonia.
Coccidioidomycosis (*Coccidioides immitis*) see page 52	7–21 days	Fever, dry cough, dyspnea, chest pain, and fatigue. Weight loss, migratory arthralgias and headache are also common. CXR often demonstrates unilateral infiltrates, effusions, and hilar adenopathy. Pulmonary nodules and cavitations may also be seen occasionally. Rash is common, with early fine papular, nonpruritic rash progressing to erythema nodosum and/or erythema multiforme (consider this diagnosis in the triad of fever, erythema nodosum, and arthralgias). May progress to superficial maculopapular lesions, cutaneous ulcers, subcutaneous abscesses, and/or lymphadenopathy.
Tularemia (pneumonic) (*Francisella tularensis*) see page 106	1–21 days	Sudden onset of high fever, chills, cough, prostration, headache, and substernal chest pain. Possible superficial regional adenopathy. Progresses to dyspnea, possible hemoptysis, tracheitis, bronchitis, pleural effusions, and/or pneumonia. Hilar adenopathy may be present on CXR. Can lead to respiratory failure and lung abscess.

CXR = chest x-ray

Fever with Petechiae

Disease/Agent	Incubation	Initial Symptoms
Dengue fever and **Dengue hemorrhagic fever (DHF)** (Flavivirus) see page 56	3–7 days	Sudden onset of fever, chills, malaise, arthralgias, myalgias, severe frontal headache, flushing, prominent low back pain, and dysesthesia of the skin. Often includes prostration, GI symptoms, hepatitis, macular or scarlatiniform rash, petechiae, and mucosal bleeding. May progress to DHF with hypotension, restlessness, diaphoresis, diffuse petechiae and ecchymosis, mucosal and GI bleeding, ascites, organomegaly, cyanosis, and sudden shock.
Hantavirus hemorrhagic fever with renal syndrome see page 64	5–24 days	Sudden onset of fever, chills, myalgias, headache, dizziness, low back pain, abdominal pain, conjunctival injection, blurred vision, erythematous rash on trunk and face, petechiae over upper trunk and on soft palate, and sudden severe shock and death. Survivors develop 3–10 days of mucosal bleeding, oliguria or anuria, hypertension, pneumonitis, and/or pulmonary edema.
Kyasanur Forest disease (Flavivirus) see page 68	2–9 days	Sudden onset of fever, chills, headache, vomiting, severe prostration, pains in arms and legs, flushing of face (no rash), conjunctival suffusion, hepatosplenomegaly, petechiae, general lymphadenopathy and relative bradycardia. 40% of cases will develop GI and mucosal bleeding, and/or hemorrhagic pulmonary edema. 50% of patients develop neurologic sequelae following 1–3 week afebrile period.
Lassa virus & the South American viral hemorrhagic fevers (*Arenaviruses*) see page 70	3–19 days	Fever, malaise, dizziness, myalgia, dysesthesia, abdominal pain, chest pain, back pain, sore throat, headache, vomiting, cough, photophobia, conjunctival injection, flushing of face and upper trunk, and possible axillary petechiae. May progress to hypotension, facial edema, pulmonary edema, vesicular and/or petecheal rash of oropharynx, mucosal hemorrhages, and occasional pleural effusion and/or ascites.
Omsk hemorrhagic fever (Flavivirus) see page 79	2–9 days	Sudden onset of fever, chills, headache, severe prostration, pains in arms and legs, flushing of face and trunk (no rash), conjunctival suffusion, papulovesicular eruption on soft palate, cervical lymphadenopathy, and relative bradycardia. GI and mucosal bleeding, and petechiae may occur. Neurologic sequelae or rarely pneumonia may occur late.
Rocky Mountain spotted fever (*Rickettsia rickettsii*) see page 90	2–14 days	Sudden onset of high fever, chills, myalgia, headache, nausea, vomiting, diarrhea, malaise, and abdominal pain and tenderness. The classic maculopapular rash appears occasionally on day 1, in fewer than 50% of patients by day 3, and in up to 91% by day 5, after the onset of fever, then progresses to a petecheal rash.
Typhus (*R. typhi, R. prowazekii, & Orienta tsutsugamuchi*) see page 108	6–18 days	Sudden onset of fever, chills, severe headache, and myalgia. Macular, maculopapular and/or petecheal rash usually develops by day 5.
Yellow fever (Flavivirus) see page 110	3–6 days	Sudden onset of fever, chills, headache, malaise, myalgia, facial flushing, prominent low back pain, conjunctival injection, and relative bradycardia. A diffuse petecheal and purpuric rash may occur.

GI = gastrointestinal

Cutaneous Lesions or Ulcerations

Disease/Agent	Incubation	Initial Symptoms
Anthrax, cutaneous (*Bacillus anthracis*) see page 38	1–6 days	Initially, a small pruritic group or ring of papules that evolve to vesicles and a small ulcer by the second day. Progresses to a depressed black eschar (usually 2–3 cm in size) over 2–5 days. Primarily affects hands, forearms, head, & neck, but may involve chest, eyes, and mouth.
Blastomycosis (*Blastomyces dermatitidis*) see page 42	30–45 days	Two types of skin lesions occur on exposed skin of face and extremities; small papulopustular lesions that become heaped-up crusted lesions with a gray to violaceous color, and small pustules that progress to superficial ulcers with a friable granulomatous base. Simultaneous cutaneous and pulmonary forms in 35% of cases. 19% of cases cutaneous only. Pulmonary form causes productive cough, hemoptysis, weight loss, pleuritic chest pain, low-grade fever, dyspnea, and CXR findings of pulmonary infiltrates, nodules, and/or cavitations. Hilar adenopathy may also be present.
Coccidioidomycosis (*Coccidioides immitis*) see page 52	7–21 days	Fever, dry cough, dyspnea, chest pain, and fatigue. Weight loss, migratory arthralgias and headache are also common. CXR often demonstrates unilateral infiltrates, effusions, and hilar adenopathy. Pulmonary nodules and cavitations may also occasionally be seen. Rash is common, with early fine papular, nonpruritic rash progressing to erythema nodosum and/or erythema multiforme (consider this diagnosis in the triad of fever, erythema nodosum, and arthralgias). May progress to superficial maculopapular lesions, cutaneous ulcers, subcutaneous abscesses, and/or lymphadenopathy.
Plague, bubonic (*Yersinia pestis*) see page 80	1–6 days	Fulminant onset with high fever, chills, headache, extreme malaise, and myalgia. Cough and hemoptysis are common. A small pustule or other skin lesion often appears at the site of the initial fleabite (usually on lower extremity). Nausea, vomiting, and abdominal pain may also occur. Rapidly progresses to severe pneumonia with respiratory failure, and circulatory collapse.
Smallpox (*Variola major*) see page 98	3–17 days	Initial flulike illness followed by rash 2–4 days after onset of fever. Rash usually begins on forehead and upper arms. Spreads centrally to trunk over 1–2 days. All lesions always at same stage of development (as opposed to chickenpox). Rash appears as macules and small papules (day 1–2) ⟶ papules (day 3–4) ⟶ vesicles (day 4–6) ⟶ pustules that may be umbilicated (day 7–10) ⟶ flattening of pustules (day 11) ⟶ crusting & scabbing (day 12–14). Lesions feel hard, like buckshot under the skin, are painful, and are of variable sizes.
Tularemia (*Francisella tularensis*) see page 106	1–21 days	**Ulceroglandular tularemia** is the most common natural form and presents as an erythematous and tender skin papule or 1–2 cm vesiculated lesion at the site of inoculation. Over the next several days the lesion progresses to a skin ulceration with a necrotic granulomatous base or eschar surrounded by a raised, indurated, erythematous border. A flulike illness along with regional adenopathy often begins within 3 days after the skin lesion appears. Following an aerosol release, pneumonic and typhoidal tularemia would tend to predominate.
Typhus (scrub) (*Orienta tsutsugamuchi*) see page 108	6–18 days	Sudden onset of flulike illness with fever, chills, severe headache, and myalgia. Associated with a papule at the site of inoculation (chigger bite) that progresses to an ulceration with a black crust or eschar that must be differentiated from cutaneous anthrax. Tender regional or general lymphadenopathy is common.

CXR = chest x-ray

Acute Respiratory Syndrome with Fever

Disease/Agent	Incubation	Initial Symptoms
Anthrax, inhalational (*Bacillus anthracis*) see page 38	1–6 days	24–48 hours of fever (or recent history of fever), chills, cough, malaise, headache, myalgias, and possible chest tightness. Malaise may be profound and notable. Progresses to high fever, extreme fatigue, non-productive cough, dyspnea, severe respiratory distress, cyanosis, septicemia, and death.
Blastomycosis (*Blastomyces dermatitidis*) see page 42	30–45 days	Sudden onset of fever, chills, myalgia, arthralgia, cough, and fatigue. 60% develop productive cough, hemoptysis, pleuritic chest pain, low-grade fever, dyspnea, and CXR findings of infiltrates, nodules and/or cavitations.
Coccidioidomycosis (*Coccidioides immitis*) see page 52	7–21 days	Fever, dry cough, dyspnea, chest pain, and fatigue. Weight loss, migratory arthralgias and headache are also common. CXR often demonstrates unilateral infiltrates, effusions and hilar adenopathy. Pulmonary nodules and cavitations may also occasionally be seen. Rash is common, with early fine papular, nonpruritic rash progressing to erythema nodosum and/or erythema multiforme (consider this diagnosis in the triad of fever, erythema nodosum, and arthralgias). May progress to superficial maculopapular lesions, cutaneous ulcers, subcutaneous abscesses, and/or lymphadenopathy.
Glanders (*Burkholderia mallei*) see page 62	3–14 days	Sudden onset of fever, rigors, sweats, cough, myalgias, pleuritic chest pain, photophobia, lacrimation, diarrhea, tachycardia, cervical adenopathy, and mild splenomegaly. Pneumonia may or may not be present at this stage. With septicemia, may produce a papular or papulopustular rash that can be mistaken for smallpox.
Hantavirus pulmonary syndrome see page 64	5–24 days	Sudden onset of fever, chills, myalgias, headache, dizziness, dry cough, nausea, vomiting, and other gastrointestinal symptoms. Malaise, diarrhea, and lightheadedness in 50% of all cases. Progresses to dyspnea, rales, tachycardia, tachypnea, and possible hypotension. There is pulmonary edema, ARDS, and death in about 50% of victims.
Legionnaires' disease (*Legionella pneumophila*) see page 72	2–10 days	Fever, chills, malaise, myalgias, headache, dry cough, dizziness, and nausea. Progresses to atypical pneumonia, mildly productive cough, possible hemoptysis, rales, chest pain, and occasional nausea, vomiting, diarrhea, and abdominal pain.
Leptospirosis (*Leptospira* species) see page 74	3–30 days	Sudden onset of remittent fever,* chills or rigors, headache, myalgia, low back pain, and conjunctival injection. May also include cough, abdominal pain, nausea, vomiting, diarrhea, pharyngitis, and/or a pretibial maculopapular rash. May progress to high fever, liver failure, acute renal failure, aseptic meningitis, pneumonitis with hemoptysis, ARDS, bleeding diathesis, cardiac arrhythmias, shock, and death.
Melioidosis (*Burkholderia pseudomallei*) see page 76	2 days to years	Sudden onset of high fever, chills, productive or nonproductive cough, headache, myalgias, chest pain, and anorexia. May progress to pneumonia and/or acute lung abscesses.
Plague, pneumonic (*Yersinia pestis*) see page 80	1–6 days	Fulminant onset with high fever, chills, headache, extreme malaise, and myalgia. Cough and hemoptysis are common. Nausea, vomiting, and abdominal pain may also occur. Rapidly progresses to severe pneumonia with respiratory failure and circulatory collapse.

Acute Respiratory Syndrome with Fever

Psittacosis (*Chlamydia psittaci*) see page 82	5–15 days	Gradual or fulminant onset of fever, chills, myalgias, malaise, chest pain, & dry, hacking cough. Rales and hepatomegaly often present. Relative bradycardia is common. CXR usually shows miliary, patchy, or diffuse infiltrates or nodular, segmental, or lobar consolidation. Cervical adenopathy may be present, and a maculopapular rash occurs rarely.
Q fever (*Coxiella burnetii*) see page 84	2–14 days	High fever, chills, malaise, fatigue, headache, anorexia, and myalgias. Atypical pneumonia in 50% of infected patients with cough, chest pain, and rales in 25% of infected patients after 4–5 days of illness.
Ricin (castor bean extract) & **abrin** (rosary pea extract) see page 86	4–8 hr	Fever, cough, dyspnea, chest tightness, cyanosis, abdominal pain, nausea, vomiting, and gastrointestinal hemorrhage with hematemesis and hematochezia. May progress to pulmonary edema, ARDS, necrosis of the liver, spleen, and/or kidneys, and shock.
Staphylococcal enterotoxin B see page 101	3–12 hr	Sudden onset of fever, chills, headache, myalgia, and nonproductive cough. Severe intoxication may produce dyspnea, retrosternal chest pain, nausea, vomiting, diarrhea, dehydration and hypotension. May progress to pulmonary edema and/or ARDS.
Tularemia (pneumonic) (*Francisella tularensis*) see page 106	1–21 days	Sudden onset of high fever, chills, cough, prostration, headache, and substernal chest pain. Possible superficial regional adenopathy. Progresses to dyspnea, possible hemoptysis, tracheitis, bronchitis, pleural effusions, and/or pneumonia. Can lead to respiratory failure and lung abscess.

*Remittent fevers are those that go up and down without ever returning to normal, as opposed to **intermittent fevers**, which are elevated with irregular returns to normal, and **relapsing fevers,** which are elevated with regular returns to normal.

Acute Respiratory Syndrome without Fever

Disease/Agent	Incubation	Initial Symptoms
Trichothecene (T-2) mycotoxins, inhalation see page 104	Minutes to hours	Skin itching and burning pain, redness & blistering, anorexia, nausea, vomiting, crampy abdominal pain, watery and/or bloody diarrhea, arthralgias, nasal itching and pain, sneezing, epistaxis, rhinorrhea, mouth and/or throat pain, cough, dyspnea, chest pain, wheezing, and hemoptysis.

Flulike Illness with Rash

Disease/Agent	Incubation	Initial Symptoms
Alkhurma virus (see Kyasanur Forest disease) see page 68	2–8 days	Biphasic illness with 1–3 week afebrile period between phases. Phase 1 consists of 6–11 days of fever, chills, headache, vomiting, severe prostration, arthralgia, myalgia, facial flushing, conjunctival suffusion, hepatosplenomegaly, petechiae, general lymphadenopathy and relative bradycardia. There may be a measles-like rash on hands, feet, and trunk. 40% develop GI and mucosal hemorrhage. Phase 2 consists of meningoencephalitis with delirium, convulsions, and/or coma.
Blastomycosis (*Blastomyces dermatitidis*) see page 42	30–45 days	Sudden onset of fever, chills, myalgia, arthralgia, cough, and fatigue. Development of small papulopustular lesions that become heaped-up crusted lesions with a gray to violaceous color **or** small pustules that progress to superficial ulcers with a friable granulomatous base. Pulmonary symptoms in 35% of cases.
Chikungunya (*Alphavirus*) see page 48	1–12 days	Abrupt onset of high fever, chills, severe headache, retro-orbital pain, flushing of face and trunk followed by a maculopapular rash of trunk and extremities, and migratory small joint arthralgias (hands, wrists, ankles & feet primarily), which may be severe. A dengue hemorrhagic fever–like syndrome may occur rarely, especially in children.
Coccidioidomycosis (*Coccidioides immitis*) see page 52	7–21 days	Fever, dry cough, dyspnea, chest pain, and fatigue. Weight loss, migratory arthralgias, and headache are also common. CXR often demonstrates unilateral infiltrates, effusions, and hilar adenopathy. Pulmonary nodules and cavitations may also occasionally be seen. Rash is common, with early fine papular, nonpruritic rash progressing to erythema nodosum and/or erythema multiforme (consider this diagnosis in the triad of fever, erythema nodosum, and arthralgias). May progress to superficial maculopapular lesions, cutaneous ulcers, subcutaneous abscesses, and/or lymphadenopathy.
Dengue fever (*Flavivirus*) see page 56	4–7 days	Sudden onset of fever, chills, malaise, myalgias, severe frontal headache, retro-orbital pain, flushing, prominent low back pain, and dysesthesia and/or hyperesthesia of the skin. Symptoms may also include prostration, abdominal tenderness, nausea, vomiting, anorexia, hepatitis, and generalized flushing that progress to a macular or scarlatiniform rash over 3–4 days (sparing palms and soles). Petechiae and mucosal bleeding may also be present.
Ebola & Marburg viral hemorrhagic fevers (*Filoviridae*) see page 59	3–14 days	Sudden onset of fever, chills, headache, myalgia, generalized weakness, prostration, cough, sore throat, and conjunctivitis. A maculopapular rash may develop about day 5.
Glanders (*Burkholderia mallei*) see page 62	3–14 days	Sudden onset of fever, rigors, sweats, cough, myalgias, pleuritic chest pain, photophobia, lacrimation, diarrhea, tachycardia, cervical adenopathy, and mild splenomegaly. Pneumonia may or may not be present at this stage. With septicemia, may produce a papular or papulopustular rash that can be mistaken for smallpox.
Leptospirosis (*Leptospira* species) see page 74	3–30 days	Sudden onset of remittent fever, chills or rigors, headache, myalgia, low back pain, and conjunctival injection. Fewer than 50% of initial cases will also demonstrate cough, abdominal pain, nausea, vomiting, diarrhea, pharyngitis, and/or a pretibial maculopapular rash.

Flulike Illness with Rash

Plague, pneumonic (*Yersinia pestis*) see page 80	1–6 days	Fulminant onset with high fever, chills, headache, extreme malaise, and myalgia. Within 24 hr there is often cough and hemoptysis. There may also be nausea, vomiting, and abdominal pain. Rapidly progresses to severe pneumonia.
Psittacosis (*Chlamydia psittaci*) see page 82	5–15 days	Gradual or fulminant onset of fever, chills, myalgias, malaise, chest pain, & dry, hacking cough. Rales and hepatomegaly often present. Relative bradycardia is common. CXR usually shows miliary, patchy, or diffuse infiltrates, or nodular, segmental, or lobar consolidation. Cervical adenopathy may be present, and a maculopapular rash occurs rarely.
Rocky Mountain spotted fever (*Rickettsia rickettsii*) see page 90	2–14 days	Sudden onset of high fever, chills, myalgia, headache, nausea, vomiting, diarrhea, malaise, and abdominal pain and tenderness. The classic maculopapular rash appears occasionally on day 1, in fewer than 50% of patients by day 3, and in up to 91% by day 5, after the onset of fever.
Smallpox (*Variola major*) see page 98	3–19 days	Sudden onset of fever, malaise, headache, backache, chills/rigors, and vomiting. Occasionally includes pharyngitis, delirium in adults, abdominal pain, erythematous (measles-like) rash, diarrhea, and seizures in children.
Typhoid and paratyphoid fevers (*Salmonella typhi* and *Salmonella paratyphi*) see page 92	5–21 days	Acute or gradual onset of abdominal tenderness and fever. Diarrhea or constipation may precede onset of fever by several days, along with chills, diaphoresis, headache, anorexia, cough, weakness, sore throat, dizziness, and/or myalgia. Rose-colored maculopapular rash on trunk in 30% of victims.
Typhus (*R. typhi, R. prowazekii, & Orienta tsutsugamuchi*) see page 108	6–18 days	Sudden onset of fever, chills, severe headache, and myalgia. Macular, maculopapular, and/or petechial rash usually develops by day 5
Yellow fever (*Flavivirus*) see page 110	3–6 days	Sudden onset of fever, chills, headache, malaise, myalgia, facial flushing, prominent low back pain, conjunctival injection, and relative bradycardia. A diffuse petechial and purpuric rash may occur.

CXR = chest x-ray; GI = gastrointestinal

Fever with Lymphadenopathy

Disease/Agent	Incubation	Initial Symptoms
Coccidioidomycosis (*Coccidioides immitis*) see page 52	7–21 days	Fever, dry cough, dyspnea, chest pain, and fatigue. Weight loss, migratory arthralgias, and headache are also common. CXR often demonstrates unilateral infiltrates, effusions, and hilar adenopathy. Pulmonary nodules and cavitations may also occasionally be seen. Rash is common, with early fine papular, nonpruritic rash progressing to erythema nodosum and/or erythema multiforme (consider this diagnosis in the triad of fever, erythema nodosum, and arthralgias). May progress to superficial maculopapular lesions, cutaneous ulcers, subcutaneous abscesses, and/or lymphadenopathy.
Glanders (*Burkholderia mallei*) see page 62	3–14 days	Sudden onset of fever, rigors, sweats, cough, myalgias, pleuritic chest pain, photophobia, lacrimation, diarrhea, tachycardia, cervical adenopathy, and mild splenomegaly. Pneumonia may or may not be present at this stage.
Kyasanur forest disease (Flavivirus) see page 68	2–9 days	Sudden onset of fever, chills, headache, vomiting, severe prostration, pains in arms and legs, flushing of face (no rash), conjunctival suffusion, hepatosplenomegaly, petechiae, general lymphadenopathy, and relative bradycardia. 40% of cases will develop GI and mucosal bleeding and/or hemorrhagic pulmonary edema. 50% of patients develop neurologic sequelae following 1–3 week afebrile period.
Melioidosis (*Burholderia pseudomallei*) see page 76	2 days to years	Acute localized melioidosis produces an acute localized infection producing a nodule or pustule at the site of infection. May be associated with lymphadenitis and regional adenopathy. Systemic symptoms include fever, chills, and myalgias. May rapidly progress to septicemic form.
Omsk hemorrhagic fever (Flavivirus) see page 79	2–9 days	Sudden onset of fever, chills, headache, severe prostration, pains in arms and legs, flushing of face and trunk (no rash), conjunctival suffusion, papulovesicular eruption on soft palate, cervical lymphadenopathy, and relative bradycardia. GI and mucosal bleeding, and petechiae may occur. Neurologic sequelae or rarely pneumonia may occur late.
Plague, bubonic (*Yersinia pestis*) see page 80	1–6 days	One or more enlarged, tender, regional lymph nodes (buboes) often in the inguinal area, extreme malaise, headache, and high fever. There may also be tender hepatosplenomegaly and a small pustule or other skin lesion at the site of the initial fleabite (usually on the lower extremity). Often progresses to septicemic plague in about 3 days.
Psittacosis (*Chlamydia psittaci*) see page 82	5–15 days	Gradual or fulminant onset of fever, chills, myalgias, malaise, chest pain, & dry, hacking cough. Rales and hepatomegaly often are present. Relative bradycardia is common. CXR usually shows miliary, patchy, or diffuse infiltrates, or nodular, segmental, or lobar consolidation. Cervical adenopathy may be present, and a maculopapular rash occurs rarely.
Tularemia, pneumonic (*Francisella tularensis*) see page 106	1–21 days	Sudden onset of high fever, chills, cough, prostration, headache, and substernal chest pain. There may or may not be superficial regional adenopathy. Rales may be present on lung exam.
Typhus, scrub (*Orienta tsutsugamuchi*) see page 108	6–18 days	A papule at the site of inoculation that progresses to an ulceration with a black crust or eschar that must be differentiated from cutaneous anthrax. Tender regional or general lymphadenopathy is common. Other associated symptom at onset may include ocular pain, conjunctival injection, dry cough, and relative bradycardia.

CXR = chest x-ray; GI = gastrointestinal

Acute Neurologic Syndrome with Fever

Disease/Agent	Incubation	Initial Symptoms
Kyasanur Forest disease (Flavivirus) see page 68	2–9 days	Sudden onset of fever, chills, headache, vomiting, severe prostration, pains in arms and legs, flushing of face (no rash), conjunctival suffusion, hepatosplenomegaly, petechiae, general lymphadenopathy and relative bradycardia. 40% of cases will develop GI and mucosal bleeding and/or hemorrhagic pulmonary edema. 50% of patients develop neurologic sequelae following 1–3 week afebrile period.
Nipah virus (*Paramyxoviridae*) see page 78	Unknown	Sudden onset of flulike illness with fever, headache, nausea, vomiting, myalgia, malaise, and drowsiness. Rapidly progresses to encephalitis with focal neurologic signs including segmental myoclonus, tremor, ptosis, ataxia, alteration of consciousness, seizures, pinpoint pupils, and hypotension.
Omsk hemorrhagic fever (Flavivirus) see page 79	2–9 days	Sudden onset of fever, chills, headache, severe prostration, pains in arms and legs, flushing of face and trunk (no rash), conjunctival suffusion, papulovesicular eruption on soft palate, cervical lymphadenopathy, and relative bradycardia. GI and mucosal bleeding, and petechiae may occur. Neurologic sequelae or rarely pneumonia may occur late.
Q fever (*Coxiella burnetii*) see page 84	2–14 days	High fever, chills, malaise, fatigue, headache, anorexia, and myalgias. Atypical pneumonia in 50% of infected patients. Rarely progresses to culture-negative endocarditis, osteomyelitis aseptic meningitis, and encephalitis.
Rocky Mountain spotted fever (*Rickettsia rickettsii*) see page 90	2–14 days	Sudden onset of flulike illness with high fever, chills, myalgia, headache, nausea, vomiting, diarrhea, malaise, and abdominal pain and tenderness. Maculopapular rash that becomes petechial. May progress to restlessness, irritability, meningismus, photophobia, lethargy, delirium, and/or coma.
Typhoid & paratyphoid fevers (*Salmonella typhi and paratyphi*) see page 92	5–21 days	Acute or gradual onset of abdominal tenderness and fever. Diarrhea or constipation may precede onset of fever by several days, along with chills, diaphoresis, headache, anorexia, cough, weakness, sore throat, dizziness, and/or myalgias. 30% will develop a faint rose-colored maculopapular rash on the trunk, and 5–10% will develop psychosis and confusion ("muttering delirium" and "coma vigil").
Smallpox (*Variola major*) see page 98	3–19 days	Sudden onset of fever, malaise, headache, backache, chills/ rigors, and vomiting. Occasionally includes pharyngitis, delirium in adults, abdominal pain, erythematous (measles-like) rash, diarrhea, and seizures in children.
Typhus (all forms) (*R. prowazekii, R. typhi* and *Orienta tsutsugamuchi*) see page 108	7 days	Sudden onset of fever, chills, severe headache, and myalgia. A macular, maculopapular, and/or petechial rash develops. CNS symptoms such as confusion, delirium, stupor, apathy, nervousness, meningismus, or coma can occur during the second week of illness.
Viral encephalitis (Venezuelan equine encephalitis) see page 60	2–6 days	Sudden onset of spiking fevers, rigors, malaise, severe headache, photophobia, and myalgias in the low back and legs. Nausea, vomiting, sore throat, cough, and diarrhea may quickly follow the initial onset. May progress to meningismus, lethargy, somnolence, ataxia, confusion, seizures, paralysis, coma, or death.

CNS = central nervous system; GI = gastrointestinal

Acute Neurologic Syndrome without Fever

Disease/Agent	Incubation	Initial Symptoms
Botulinum toxin (*Clostridium botulinum*) see page 44	12–36 hr	Initially blurred vision, mydriasis, diplopia, ptosis, photophobia, hoarseness, dysarthric speech, dysphonia, and dysphagia. Progresses to descending, symmetrical skeletal muscle paralysis and respiratory arrest. Patients remain afebrile.
Domoic acid (amnesic shellfish poisoning) see page 58	3–24 hr	Nausea, vomiting, diarrhea, abdominal cramping, and severe headache occur initially. Progresses to confusion, hyporeflexia, short-term memory loss, disorientation, motor weakness, and mental status varying from agitation to coma. Seizures, profuse respiratory secretions and cardiac arrhythmias may also be present.
Saxitoxin (paralytic shellfish poisoning) see page 94	30 min–10 hr	Initially brief nausea and vomiting, followed by paresthesias of the mouth, lips, face, and extremities. Diarrhea may also be present. In severe intoxications progresses to dyspnea, dysphagia, dysarthric speech, ataxia, muscle weakness, paralysis, respiratory insufficiency or failure, heart failure, cardiac arrhythmias and hypotension.
Tetrodotoxin (puffer fish toxin) see page 102	10 min–3 hr	Initially slight numbness of the lips and tongue followed by progressive paresthesias of the face and extremities, chest tightness, and dizziness or a floating sensation. Headache, salivation, diaphoresis, epigastric pain, nausea, vomiting, and diarrhea also occur commonly. May progress to diffuse weakness, unsteady gait, progressive ascending paralysis, difficulty speaking, increasing respiratory distress with dyspnea and cyanosis, and hypotension or hypertension.

KVCC KALAMAZOO VALLEY
COMMUNITY COLLEGE
LIBRARY

Acute GI Syndrome with Fever

Disease/Agent	Incubation	Initial Symptoms
Aflatoxins (*Aspergillus* species) see page 36	Days to weeks	Acute hepatic necrosis with fever, jaundice, edema of the limbs, abdominal pain, nausea, vomiting, pulmonary edema, hemorrhage, hepatomegaly, seizures, coma, and death.
Anthrax, gastrointestinal (*Bacillus anthracis*) see page 38	1–6 days	24–48 hr of fever, nausea, vomiting, and anorexia. Rapidly progresses to hematemesis, hematochezia, and symptoms of acute abdomen. May also be associated with severe pulmonary symptoms.
Brucellosis (*Brucella suis & melitensis*) see page 46	Days to months	Intermittent fever, chills, sweats, headache, myalgia, arthralgias, back pain, generalized weakness, malaise, anorexia, nausea, vomiting, diarrhea and/or constipation. Cough and pleuritic chest pain in up to 20% of patients.
Cholera (*Vibrio cholerae*) see page 50	4 hr–5 days	Sudden onset of abdominal cramping, painless watery diarrhea, vomiting, malaise, and headache. Low-grade fever may or may not be present. Progresses to profuse, thin, mucousy, gray-brown (rice-water) diarrhea of up to 1 L per hour.
Dengue fever (Flavivirus) see page 56	3–7 days	Sudden onset of fever, chills, malaise, myalgias, severe frontal headache, flushing, prominent low back pain, and dysesthesia of the skin. May also include prostration, abdominal tenderness, nausea, vomiting, anorexia, hepatitis, and a macular or scarlatiniform rash. Petechiae and mucosal bleeding may also be present.
Domoic acid (amnesic shellfish poisoning) see page 58	3–24 hr	Nausea, vomiting, diarrhea, abdominal cramping, and severe headache occur initially. Progresses to neurologic symptoms, including short-term memory loss, confusion, disorientation, weakness, and seizures.
Ebola & Marburg viral hemorrhagic fevers (Filoviridae) see page 59	3–14 days	Sudden onset of fever, chills, headache, myalgia, generalized weakness, prostration, cough, sore throat, and conjunctivitis. May progress to nausea, vomiting, diarrhea, abdominal pain, photophobia, maculopapular rash, DIC, internal and external hemorrhages, and multiorgan failure.
Leptospirosis (*Leptospira* species) see page 74	3–30 days	Sudden onset of remittent fever, chills or rigors, headache, myalgia, low back pain, and conjunctival injection. Fewer than 50% of initial cases will also demonstrate cough, abdominal pain, nausea, vomiting, diarrhea, pharyngitis, and/or a pretibial maculopapular rash.
Ricin (castor bean extract) & **abrin** (rosary pea extract), **ingestion only** see page 86	4–8 hr	Abdominal pain, nausea, vomiting, and gastrointestinal hemorrhage with hematemesis and hematochezia. May progress to necrosis of the liver, spleen, and/or kidneys and shock.
Salmonella nontyphoidal gastroenteritis see page 92	6–48 hr	Acute onset of nausea, vomiting, diarrhea, low-grade fever, chills, and abdominal cramping. Myalgia and malaise may also occur.
Shigellosis (*Shigella dysenteriae* 1) see page 96	1–3 days	Abdominal pain, cramping, and fever, followed by voluminous watery diarrhea. This progresses to bloody mucoid stools, urgency, tenesmus, toxemia with high fever, and abdominal tenderness.
Staphylococcal enterotoxin B see page 101	3–12 hr	Sudden onset of fever, chills, headache, myalgia, and nonproductive cough. Severe intoxication may produce dyspnea, retrosternal chest pain, nausea, vomiting, diarrhea, dehydration, and hypotension.

Acute GI Syndrome with Fever

Tularemia (*Francisella* *tularensis*) see page 106	1–21 days	Sudden onset of high fever, chills, cough, prostration, headache, and substernal chest pain. Possible superficial regional adenopathy. Progresses to dyspnea, possible hemoptysis, tracheitis, bronchitis, pleural effusions, and/or pneumonia. Nausea, vomiting, & diarrhea likely from swallowed organisms after bioterrorism attack.
Typhoid and paratyphoid fevers (*Salmonella typhi* and *paratyphi*) see page 92	5–21 days	Acute or gradual onset of abdominal tenderness and fever. Diarrhea or constipation may precede onset of fever by several days, along with chills, diaphoresis, headache, anorexia, cough, weakness, sore throat, dizziness, and/or myalgia.
Viral encephalitis (Venezuelan equine encephalitis) see page 60	2–6 days	Sudden onset of spiking fevers, rigors, malaise, severe headache, photophobia, and myalgias in the low back and legs. Nausea, vomiting, diarrhea, sore throat, & cough may quickly follow the initial onset. May progress to meningismus, lethargy, somnolence, ataxia, confusion, seizures, paralysis, coma, and death,
Yellow fever (*Flavivirus*) see page 110	3–7 days	Sudden onset of fever, chills, headache, malaise, myalgia, facial flushing, low back pain, and conjunctival injection. May progress to nausea, vomiting, abdominal pain, somnolence, weakness and prostration, hepatitis with jaundice, ascites, and hemorrhagic diathesis.

DIC = disseminated intravascular coagulation; GI = gastrointestinal

Acute GI Syndrome without Fever

Disease/Agent	Incubation	Initial Symptoms
Cholera (*Vibrio cholerae*) see page 50	4 hr–5 days	Sudden onset of abdominal cramping, painless watery diarrhea, vomiting, malaise, and headache. Low-grade fever may or may not be present. Progresses to profuse, watery, gray-brown (rice-water) diarrhea of up to 1 L per hour.
Domoic acid (amnesic shellfish poisoning) see page 58	3–24 hr	Nausea, vomiting, diarrhea, abdominal cramping, and severe headache occur initially. Progresses to neurologic symptoms including short-term memory loss, confusion, disorientation, weakness, and seizures.
Ricin (castor bean extract) & **Abrin** (rosary pea extract), **ingestion only** see page 86	4–8 hr	Abdominal pain, nausea, vomiting, and GI hemorrhage with hematemesis and hematochezia. May progress to necrosis of the liver, spleen, and/or kidneys and shock.
Saxitoxin (paralytic shellfish poisoning) see page 94	30 min–10 hr	Initially brief nausea and vomiting, followed by paresthesias of the mouth, lips, face, and extremities. Diarrhea may also be present. In severe intoxications progresses to dyspnea, dysphagia, dysarthric speech, ataxia, muscle weakness, paralysis, respiratory insufficiency or failure, heart failure, cardiac arrhythmias, and hypotension.
Tetrodotoxin (puffer fish toxin) see page 102	10 min–3 hr	Initially slight numbness of the lips and tongue followed by progressive paresthesias of the face and extremities, chest tightness, and dizziness or a floating sensation. Headache, salivation, diaphoresis, epigastric pain, nausea, vomiting, and diarrhea also occur commonly. May progress to diffuse neurologic symptoms with ascending paralysis.
Trichothecene (T-2) mycotoxins, ingestion see page 104	Minutes to hours	Anorexia, nausea, vomiting, crampy abdominal pain, and watery and/or bloody diarrhea. Usually accompanied by upper and lower respiratory symptoms, eye irritation, and skin redness and/or blistering (following inhalation).

GI = gastrointestinal

INDIVIDUAL BIOLOGICAL WEAPON DETAILED

QUICK REFERENCES

A Detailed Quick Reference for

Aflatoxins

OVERVIEW   Aflatoxins are a class of toxins produced by several strains of the common fungus *Aspergillus* (mostly *A. flavus* and *A. parasiticus*). Natural human and animal intoxication occurs from ingesting contaminated grains and nuts such as corn, wheat, Brazil nuts, pecans, pistachio nuts, walnuts, and peanuts, especially when grown during times of drought. In a bioterrorist attack, aflatoxins would most likely be released as an aerosol or droplets with **intoxication of the victims occurring by inhalation, ingestion, and/or direct absorption through the skin.** The single dose LD_{50} of aflatoxin ranges from 0.5 to 10 mg/kg. **Aflatoxin is known to have been weaponized by the Iraqi biowarfare program.**

INCUBATION (LATENT) PERIOD   The incubation period is very variable and related to dose and route. It probably lasts for days or weeks. **Person-to-person transmission does not occur.**

Symptoms and Clinical Course[3,24]

- Initial presentation in a large initial exposure is related to acute hepatic necrosis and consists of fever, jaundice, edema of the limbs, abdominal pain, nausea, vomiting, pulmonary edema, hemorrhage, hepatomegaly, seizures, coma, and death. In two described outbreaks, the initial mortality rates were 27% and 60%.
- Survivors may progress to fatty liver, cirrhosis, and/or hepatic carcinoma. Pulmonary adenomatosis may occur following inhalational exposure. Many victims recover without apparent sequelae.

DIAGNOSIS[3,24]   Clinical suspicion is critical, and aflatoxin intoxication should be considered in any cluster of patients with an unexplained acute hepatitis–like illness.

- It must be differentiated from other forms of chemical, toxic, and viral hepatitis.
- An enzyme linked immunosorbent assay (ELISA) has been used to identify aflatoxin B1 in human urine, but it is not generally available.

TREATMENT[3]   There is no specific treatment or antidote.

- Initiate symptomatic and supportive care only.
- Administer activated charcoal following oral ingestion.
- Check liver function tests at regular intervals as clinically dictated.
- Decontamination of patients' skin will usually not be necessary, but if required by the presence of residual agent, use only soap and water.

ISOLATION PRECAUTIONS   Use standard precautions (gloves, hand washing, and splash precautions, as needed).

A Detailed Quick Reference for

Anthrax (Inhalational and Gastrointestinal)

OVERVIEW   *Bacillus anthracis* is an encapsulated, gram-positive, spore-forming bacillus. Spores can survive for decades and are resistant to heat, microwaves, and ultraviolet light. It kills by production of toxins, with nearly 100% mortality if untreated. There are three forms: inhalational, gastrointestinal (GI), and cutaneous, depending on the route of exposure. It may rarely produce a fatal anthrax meningitis.

INCUBATION PERIOD AND SPREAD   Incubation is 1–13 days (rarely up to 60 days) for the inhalational form and 3 to 5 days for gastrointestinal anthrax. **No person-to-person transmission of inhalational or GI anthrax has been documented**. GI anthrax is acquired by ingestion of contaminated food. **Inhalational anthrax is the most likely form following an aerosol release in a bioterrorism attack**. About 10,000 spores (possibly as few as 100) may produce lethal infection.

SYMPTOMS AND CLINICAL COURSE[3,6,21,26]
- **Inhalational anthrax**: Initial presentation includes 24–48 hr of nonspecific flulike illness with fever, chills, cough, headache, myalgias, malaise (often profound), and dyspnea. It may also include chest tightness or pleuritic pain. Nasal congestion, rhinorrhea, and/or sore throat are uncommon (<20%). Progresses to high fever, extreme fatigue, nonproductive cough, diaphoresis, severe respiratory distress, cyanosis, septicemia, and death.
- **Gastrointestinal anthrax**: Initial presentation of the intestinal form includes 24–48 hr of fever, nausea, vomiting, and anorexia. Rapidly progresses to hematemesis, hematochezia, and symptoms of acute abdomen (abdominal pain, tenderness, guarding and rebound).
- Without treatment, mortality is nearly 100% from toxemia, sepsis, and septic shock.
- **Treatment of both forms is usually futile after predromic period (1–2 days).**
- Anthrax may also produce an **oral-pharyngeal** form with oral and/or esophageal ulcers and regional lymphadenopathy. It has an untreated mortality rate of 50–60%.

DIAGNOSIS[3,6,21,26]   Diagnosis is based mostly on clinical presentation and history of possible exposure. Chest x-ray (CXR) may show widened mediastinum, mediastinal adenopathy, and/or pleural effusion. Infiltrates may also be present. If CXR results are uncertain, proceed to chest computed tomography (CT). Gram-positive rods can often be seen on peripheral blood smear, and blood cultures are often positive within 12 hr. Presently, PCR is available only through the Centers for Disease Control and Prevention (CDC) and certain laboratories.

EXPOSURE PROPHYLAXIS[21,25]   Treat for 60 days or until 3 doses of vaccine have been administered.
- Ciprofloxacin 500 mg (peds 10–15 mg/kg) PO Q12 hr (levofloxacin 500 mg PO Q24 hr may be an alternative) **or** doxycycline 100 mg PO Q12 hr (peds 2.5 mg/kg) Q12 hr **or** amoxicillin 500 mg PO Q8 hr (peds 40 mg/kg/day divided Q8 hr)

- Acellular vaccine (if available) 0.5 ml SQ at the time of exposure, then at 2 and 4 weeks, and 6, 12, and 18 months. The release of the vaccine for use is controlled by the CDC.

TREATMENT OF ACTIVE ANTHRAX INFECTION[21,25]   Treat for 60 days, and change IV to PO meds when the patient is stable.

- Ciprofloxacin 400 mg (peds 10–15 mg/kg) IV Q12 hr (levofloxacin 500 mg IV Q24 hr may be an alternative) **or** doxycycline 100 mg (peds 2.5 mg/kg) IV Q12 hr **PLUS** rifampin 600 mg (peds 10–20 mg/kg) PO Q day **or** clindamycin 900 mg IV Q8 hr (peds 5–10 mg/kg Q12 hr) **or** v*ancomycin* 1 g IV Q12 hr (peds: see PDR) **or** imipenem 500 mg IM or IV Q6 hr (peds: see PDR) **or** ampicillin 500 mg IV Q6 hr (peds: see PDR) **or** clarithromycin 500 mg (p 7.5 mg/kg) PO Q12 hr
- Administer standard symptomatic and supportive therapy for respiratory failure, shock, and fluid replacement.

ISOLATION PRECAUTIONS   Use standard precautions (gloves, hand washing, and splash precautions, as needed). **Decontaminate patients with soap and water only.** Spores on surfaces can be killed by 10% hypochlorite solution (1 part bleach in 9 parts water).

A Detailed Quick Reference for

Anthrax (Cutaneous)

OVERVIEW   *Bacillus anthracis* is an encapsulated, gram-positive, spore-forming bacillus. Spores can survive for decades and are resistant to heat, microwaves, and ultraviolet light. Cutaneous anthrax produces skin lesions by entry through an opening in the skin and subsequent release of toxins.

INCUBATION PERIOD AND SPREAD   The incubation period is **1–12 days for cutaneous anthrax.** Person-to-person transmission is only by direct contact with a skin lesion and may result in a secondary cutaneous infection.

SYMPTOMS AND CLINICAL COURSE[3,6,21]
- Initial presentation consists of a small pruritic group or ring of papules that evolves to vesicles and then to a small skin ulcer by the second day. Progresses to a depressed black eschar (usually 2–3 cm in size) over 2–5 days. Primarily affects hands, forearms, head, and neck, but may involve chest, eyes, and mouth. Usually resolves in about 2 weeks.
- Without proper treatment, it may lead to a fatal systemic form of anthrax in about 20% of victims. This occurs following progression to a lymphangitis and painful lymphadenopathy that progresses to septic shock.

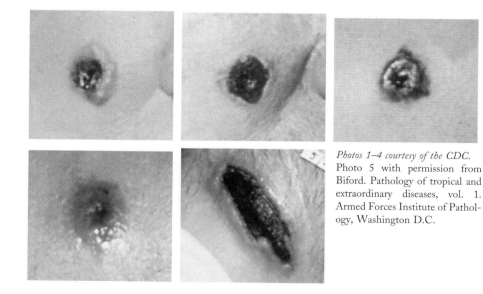

Photos 1–4 courtesy of the CDC. Photo 5 with permission from Biford. Pathology of tropical and extraordinary diseases, vol. 1. Armed Forces Institute of Pathology, Washington D.C.

DIAGNOSIS[3,6,21]   Diagnosis is mostly based on clinical presentation, appearance of the skin lesion, and a history of possible exposure. Gram-positive rods can often be seen on gram stain and/or culture of vesicular fluid. A punch biopsy can also be sent for culture, immunohistochemical staining, and/or PCR (presently available only through the CDC and certain laboratories). Blood cultures should also be obtained before instituting antibiotic therapy.

TREATMENT FOR INDIVIDUAL SMALL LESIONS AND EXPOSURE PROPHY-LAXIS[21,25]   Treat for 60 days or until 3 doses of vaccine have been administered. All patients with cutaneous anthrax following a bioterrorist attack should be presumed to have also been exposed to inhalational anthrax.
- Ciprofloxacin 500 mg (peds 10–15 mg/kg) PO Q12 hr (levofloxacin 500 mg PO Q24 hr may be an alternative) **or** doxycycline 100 mg PO Q12 hr (peds 2.5 mg/kg) PO Q12 hr **or** amoxicillin 500 mg PO Q8 hr (peds 40 mg/kg/day divided Q8 hr)
- Acellular vaccine (if available) 0.5 ml SQ at the time of exposure, then at 2 and 4 weeks, and 6, 12, and 18 months

TREATMENT FOR MULTIPLE EXTENSIVE LESIONS OR LESIONS OF THE HEAD AND NECK[21,25]   Treat for 60 days, and change IV to PO meds when patient is stable.
- Ciprofloxacin 400 mg (peds 10–15 mg/kg) IV Q12 hr (levofloxacin 500 mg IV Q24 hr may be an alternative) **or** doxycycline 100 mg (peds 2.5 mg/kg) IV Q12 hr **PLUS** rifampin 600 mg (peds 10–20 mg/kg) PO Q day **or** clindamycin 900 mg IV Q8 hr (peds 5–10 mg/kg Q12 hr) **or** vancomycin 1 g IV Q12 hr (peds: see PDR) **or** imipenem 500 mg IM/IV Q6 hr (peds: see PDR) **or** ampicillin 500 mg IV Q6 hr (peds: see PDR) **or** clarithromycin 500 mg (peds 7.5 mg/kg) PO Q12 hr

ISOLATION PRECAUTIONS   Use standard precautions (gloves, hand washing, and splash precautions, as needed). **Decontaminate patients with soap and water only.** Spores on surfaces can be killed by 10% hypochlorite solution (1 part bleach in 9 parts water).

A Detailed Quick Reference for

Blastomycosis

OVERVIEW   Blastomycosis is produced by the fungus *Blastomyces dermatitidis,* which is endemic to the southern, eastern, and central regions of North America. It produces a systemic disease with primarily pulmonary and cutaneous findings, but it may infect any organ or system. **Clinically apparent illness occurs in fewer than 50% of those with naturally acquired infection, but in a bioterrorism attack, the higher levels of spore exposure attained would likely produce illness in a greater percentage of exposed victims.** The mortality rate is about 5%.

INCUBATION PERIOD AND SPREAD   The incubation period is **30–45 days.** Infection occurs via inhalation into the lungs of spores contained in dust from organic soil. In a terrorist attack, it would be released as an aerosol, and the incubation period may be reduced as a result of higher levels of spore exposure. **Person-to-person transmission does not occur.**

SYMPTOMS AND CLINICAL COURSE[1,23]
- Initial presentation consists of sudden onset of flulike illness with fever, chills, myalgia, arthralgia, cough, and fatigue.
- May progress to
  - **Pulmonary infection** (60% of all cases) with productive cough, hemoptysis, weight loss, pleuritic chest pain, low-grade fever, and dyspnea. CXR may show findings of pulmonary infiltrates, nodules, and/or cavitations. Hilar adenopathy may also be present.
  - **Cutaneous infection** produces two types of skin lesions occurring mostly on exposed skin of the face and extremities. It may occur along with pulmonary infection:
    - Small papulopustular lesions that become heaped up and crusted, with a gray to violaceous color
    - Small pustules that progress to superficial ulcers with a friable granulomatous base
  - **Skeletal infection** produces well-demarcated lytic bone lesions with contiguous tissue abscesses (33% of all patients). It most often affects long bones, vertebrae, and ribs.

DIAGNOSIS[1,23]   Clinical suspicion is critical.
- Spherical or budding yeastlike forms may be seen in wet mount or KOH preparation of pus, sputum, secretions, and/or tissue.

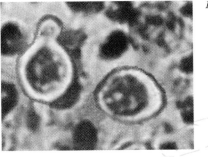

Picture courtesy of Danielle Weinstein.

- Gomori methenamine silver stain of tissue specimens.
- Specimens can be cultured on special enriched agar.
- Various immunoassays are available and are sensitive but lack specificity.

TREATMENT[1,23]   **Treat for at least 6 months.** The relapse rate is 10–14%, so recheck patients at regular intervals for 1–2 years following completion of treatment.
- **Serious non-CNS infection:** Amphotericin B 0.3–0.6 mg/kg IV Q day. When patient is stable, switch to itraconazole 200 mg PO Q day.
- **CNS infection:** Amphotericin B 0.7–1.0 mg/kg IV Q day. When patient is stable, switch to itraconazole 200 mg PO Q day.
- **Mild to moderate infection:** Itraconazole 200 mg PO Q day **or** *ketoconazole* 400 mg PO Q day.

ISOLATION PRECAUTIONS   Use standard precautions (gloves, hand washing, and splash precautions, as needed).

A Detailed Quick Reference for

Botulism (Botulinum Toxins)

OVERVIEW   Botulism is caused by a group of neurotoxins produced by the obligate anaerobic, spore-forming, gram-positive bacillus *Clostridium botulinum*. The botulinum toxins produce their effect by binding to the presynaptic nerve endings at the neuromuscular junctions and prevent the release of the neurotransmitter acetylcholine. They are, by weight, the most toxic substances known, with an LD_{50} of only .001 µg/kg. Natural intoxication occurs from eating contaminated food. **In a bioterrorism attack, botulinum toxins will most likely be released as an aerosol, although they could also be added to the food or water supply.** U.S. Army guinea pig studies from the 1940s suggest that botulinum toxins would make a less effective weapon when delivered as an aerosol.

INCUBATION (LATENT) PERIOD   The incubation period is normally **18–36 hours after ingestion or inhalation**, but it may take up to several days, depending on the size and route of exposure. The incubation period after inhalation may be longer than after ingestion. **Person-to-person transmission does not occur.**

SYMPTOMS AND CLINICAL COURSE[3,5,6]   The symptoms of intoxication are identical whether exposure is by ingestion or inhalation.
- Initial presentation consists of bulbar palsies manifested as blurred vision, mydriasis, diplopia, ptosis, photophobia, hoarseness, dysarthric speech, dysphonia, and dysphagia. Patients remain **afebrile** and may also complain of dry mouth, constipation, and urinary retention.
- Progresses to descending, symmetrical skeletal muscle paralysis in as little as 24 hr following the onset of symptoms. Progressive weakness may produce sudden respiratory arrest and death if untreated.
- Patients remain awake, alert, and oriented throughout the entire illness.

DIAGNOSIS[3,5,6]   Diagnosis is based on clinical presentation only and **must be considered in any cluster of patients with sudden weakness or paralysis without headache or fever**. It must be differentiated from other conditions such as Guillain-Barré syndrome (ascending paralysis), shellfish paralysis, tetrodotoxin, tick paralysis, myasthenia gravis, cerebrovascular accident (CVA), and atropine poisoning.

TREATMENT[2,3,5,6]
- There is an antitoxin that is effective for both food-borne and inhalational intoxication, but it **must be given prior to the onset of symptoms** or it is ineffective. The antitoxin is derived from horse serum and has the potential for serious hypersensitivity reactions in 7% of recipients. Botulinum antitoxin can be obtained from the CDC (404-639-2206 during business hours, 404-639-2888 at other times).
- Provide supportive care with mechanical ventilation and IV, or enteral nutritional support may be required for months.
- Gastric lavage and activated charcoal may be of benefit immediately following ingestion. Do not give emetic agents such as ipecac.

ISOLATION PRECAUTIONS   Use standard precautions (gloves, hand washing, and splash precautions, as needed). External decontamination is usually not required.

A Detailed Quick Reference for

Brucellosis

OVERVIEW   Primarily a disease of cattle, goats, and hogs, brucellosis is caused by any of a group of gram-negative coccobacilli called *Brucella*, but primarily by *Brucella suis* and *melitensis*. It is also known as undulant fever. As a weapon, it would most likely be released as an aerosol. Though rarely fatal (less than 5% in untreated patients), its debilitating symptoms and prolonged course would undoubedly put a great burden on the medical infrastructure following a bioterrorist attack with this agent.

INCUBATION PERIOD AND SPREAD   Brucellosis has a variable incubation period of **5–60 days.** Natural cases are acquired by ingestion of contaminated, unpasteurized dairy products or exposure to body fluids from infected animals. **Person-to-person transmission does not occur except by direct exposure to infected body fluids.**

SYMPTOMS AND CLINICAL COURSE[1,2,3,5]
- Initial presentation consists of a flulike illness with symptoms such as intermittent fevers, chills, sweats, headache, myalgias, arthralgias, back pain, generalized weakness, and malaise.
- Cough and pleuritic chest pain may occur in up to 20% of patients.
- GI symptoms occur in up to 70% of patients (mostly adults) and may include anorexia, nausea, vomiting, diarrhea and/or constipation, ileitis, colitis, and infiltrative hepatitis.
- Meningitis occurs in fewer than 5% of cases and may occur acutely at onset or appear later in the course and become chronic.
- Adenopathy, rash, and pharyngitis are more common in children.
- Progresses to lumbar pain and tenderness in 60% of cases due to osteoarticular infections of the spine. Paravertebral abscesses may occur and show up on CT scan or magnetic resonance imaging (MRI). Other joints commonly infected are the sacroiliac joints, hips, ankles, knees, and sternoclavicular joints.
- Endocarditis is rare and is the main cause of death.
- CXR is variable at all stages of the illness and may be normal or demonstrate hilar adenopathy, pleural effusions, single or miliary nodules, abscesses, and/or bronchopneumonia.

DIAGNOSIS[1,3,5]   Diagnosis is mostly based on clinical suspicion and a history of possible exposure.
- Laboratory and x-ray findings are often normal.
- CBC usually demonstrates a normal white cell count but may show anemia and thrombocytopenia.
- Early diagnosis may be strongly suggested by positive serum agglutinin titer or ELISA.
- Definitive diagnosis can be made during the acute febrile phase by positive cultures of blood (sensitivity of 15–70%) and bone marrow (sensitivity of about 92%).
- PCR may be available from the CDC or local health department.

EXPOSURE PROPHYLAXIS[1,3,5]   Treat for 3–6 weeks.

- Doxycycline 100 mg (peds 2.5 mg/kg) PO Q12 hr
- In a suspected large exposure, **ADD** rifampin 600 mg (peds 10–20 mg/kg) PO Q day.

TREATMENT[1,3,5]   **Treat for 6 weeks.**

- Doxycycline 100 mg (peds 2.5 mg/kg) PO Q12 hr **PLUS** gentamicin 1.0–1.7 mg/kg Q8 hr or 4–7 mg/kg Q day as a single dose (peds: varies by age; see PDR)
- Doxycycline 100 mg (peds 2.5 mg/kg) PO Q12 hr **PLUS** rifampin 600–900 mg (peds 10–20 mg/kg) PO Q day

ISOLATION PRECAUTIONS   Use standard precautions (gloves, hand washing, and splash precautions, as needed).

A Detailed Quick Reference for

Chikungunya

OVERVIEW Chikungunya is found primarily in Africa and Asia and is caused by an Alphavirus similar to those that cause arthropod-borne viral encephalitis, although chikungunya is not primarily a neurologic illness. The disease it causes consists of a flulike illness with a consistent triad of high fever, rash, and polyarthritis. The clinical illness it produces is difficult to distinguish from other similar Alphaviruses such as Ross River virus, o'nyong-nyong, Sindbis fever, and Mayaro virus. Chikungunya is rarely if ever fatal, making it a relatively poor choice for a weapon, but if released it could produce widespread suffering and disability, overwhelming the medical infrastructure. Aerosol transmission has not been documented, but at least one other Alphavirus (Venezuelan equine encephalitis) is known to spread by this route.

INCUBATION PERIOD AND SPREAD Incubation is **1–12 days (usually 2–3 days). Direct person-to-person transmission has not been documented**. Primates and possibly other mammals serve as the natural reservoir. Transmission of the disease is by mosquitoes, which may produce secondary cases following a terrorist attack.

SYMPTOMS AND CLINICAL COURSE[1,2,23,27]
- Initial presentation:
    - Abrupt onset of flulike illness with high remitting fever, shaking chills, myalgias, severe headache, retro-orbital pain, photophobia, rash, and often severe arthralgias. Sore throat, pharyngitis, and lymphadenopathy can also occur in some patients. The acute phase lasts 3–10 days.
    - The arthralgias are caused by a polyarticular, migratory, nondestructive arthritis affecting primarily the small joints of the hands, wrists, ankles, and feet. Larger joints are affected to a lesser extent. There may be joint swelling, but effusions are rare. Arthralgias may last for 1 week to several months following infection.
    - The rash begins as a flushing over the face and trunk, progressing to a maculopapular rash of the trunk and extremities, occasionally including the face, palms, and soles. Pruritis may be present, and young children may additionally develop urticaria. Petechiae may also be noted.
    - Young children may develop seizures and other neurologic signs.
    - A dengue hemorrhagic fever–like syndrome with mild mucosal and GI bleeding may occasionally occur, especially in children.
    - CBC will often show mild leukopenia and a relative lymphocytosis.

DIAGNOSIS[1,2,23,27] Consider chikungunya in any cluster of patients with the triad of fever, rash, and arthritis.
- Initiate ELISA for virus-specific IgM antibodies from blood.
- Virus can be recovered from blood during the first 48 hours of illness.
- PCR may become available from the CDC.

TREATMENT[1,2,23,27]

- Order rest for arthritic pains, and initiate supportive treatment with IV fluids, whole blood, and management of coagulopathy with platelets, fresh frozen plasma (FFP), and vitamin K if necessary.
- NSAIDs may be given for pain. If the arthritis is refractory to NSAIDs, chloroquin phosphate 250 mg Q 24 hr may be helpful in appropriate cases.
- Narcotic analgesics may be given for pain when NSAIDs are not sufficient.
- An untested experimental live-attenuated vaccine exists but would probably not be available.

ISOLATION PRECAUTIONS   Use standard precautions (gloves, hand washing, and splash precautions, as needed).

A Detailed Quick Reference for

Cholera

OVERVIEW   Cholera is caused by *Vibrio cholerae*, a free-living, short, curved, motile, gram-negative rod. Although it does not invade the intestinal mucosa, it releases an enterotoxin that produces a severe secretory diarrhea. It can cause a rapid loss of massive amounts of body fluids (up to 1 L/hr), leading to circulatory collapse and death. Cholera frequently causes asymptomatic infection, and in a terrorist attack, it would have to be added to the water supply in huge quantities capable of overcoming chlorination, which normally kills the organism. Both of these factors make it a poor choice for a biological weapon.

INCUBATION PERIOD AND SPREAD   Incubation varies from about **4 hours to 5 days (average 2–3 days)**, depending on the number of ingested organisms. Infection is produced only by ingestion and requires large numbers of organisms, although fewer organisms would be required in patients taking gastric acid suppression therapy. **Direct person-to-person transmission has not been documented except by the oral-fecal route.**

SYMPTOMS AND CLINICAL COURSE[1,2,5]   Initial presentation consists of the sudden onset of abdominal cramping, painless watery diarrhea, vomiting, malaise, and headache. Low-grade fever may be present. It progresses to
- Profuse, watery, gray-brown (rice-water) diarrhea. Fluid loss may approach 1 L/hr in about 5% of victims.
- There may be severe muscle cramps, particularly in the calves and thighs, due to water and electrolyte shifts.
- Without treatment, the disease lasts from 1 day to 1 week, with a mortality rate of about 50%. Death is due to massive fluid loss, volume depletion, and circulatory collapse.

DIAGNOSIS[1,2,5]   The clinical picture is usually diagnostic.
- Stool specimens show no RBCs or WBCs and almost no protein.
- Darkfield or phase contrast microscopy of stool will show highly motile vibrio.
- The organism can be cultured from stool on special media.

EXPOSURE PROPHYLAXIS[1,2,5]
- Traditional killed vaccine would be of limited value in a bioterrorist attack due to delayed onset of effect and limited protection.
- Inactivated oral vaccine (WC/rBS) presently available in Europe provides rapid short-term protection.

TREATMENT[1,2,5]   Treat with antibiotics for 3 days.
- Primary treatment depends on the rapid replacement of lost fluid and electrolytes by oral and/or IV routes. A glucose-electrolyte solution containing 1 L of water plus 20 g of glucose, 3.5 g of NaCl, 2.5 g of sodium bicarbonate and 1.5 g of KCl should be used.

- Ciprofloxacin 1 g (peds 10–15 mg/kg) PO as a single dose or 500 mg (peds 10 mg/ kg) PO Q 24 hr for 3 days **or**
- Doxycycline 300 mg PO for 1 dose or 100 mg PO bid for 3 days
- In suspected or proven tetracycline resistance, consider erythromycin 500 mg (peds 10 mg/kg) PO qid as an additional alternative to doxycycline.
- Alternative pediatric treatment may include TMP (4 mg)–SMX (20 mg) per kg Q 12 hr for 3 days.

ISOLATION PRECAUTIONS   Use standard precautions (gloves, hand washing, and splash precautions, as needed).

A Detailed Quick Reference for

Coccidioidomycosis

OVERVIEW   Coccidioidomycosis (Valley fever) is caused by the fungus *Coccidioides immitis*. This fungus grows naturally in its mycelial form in the soil of the southwestern United States, northern Mexico, and some areas of Central and South America. Human infection occurs via the inhalation of spores (arthroconidia) into the lungs and rarely by cutaneous inoculation with subsequent lymphatic spread. Once within a living host, the spores form spherules, which are the form of the organism that produces tissue infections. Subclinical or mild respiratory infections occur in up to half of all natural infections, but this might differ following a bioterrorist attack because high initial spore exposures have been documented to produce a shorter incubation period and a more severe illness, including diffuse pneumonia with respiratory failure and a septic shock–like syndrome. **The mortality rate of coccidioidomycosis is low (1–3%).**

INCUBATION PERIOD AND SPREAD   The incubation period is **7–21 days.** Most natural infection occurs by the inhalation of infected dust. **Direct person-to-person transmission does not occur.**

SYMPTOMS AND CLINICAL COURSE[1,23]
- Initial presentation:
  - Consists of fever, dry cough, dyspnea, chest pain, and fatigue. Weight loss, migratory arthralgias, and headache are also common.
  - CXR is abnormal in more than 50% of symptomatic patients with unilateral infiltrates, effusions, and hilar adenopathy. Pulmonary nodules and cavitations may be seen occasionally.
  - Rash is common, including an early fine papular, nonpruritic rash that may progress to erythema nodosum and/or erythema multiforme.
  - **The syndrome of fever, erythema nodosum, and arthralgias (desert rheumatism) should raise a suspicion of coccidioidomycosis.**
- More severe infections may induce a greater than 10% weight loss, severe night sweats of more than 3 weeks' duration, pulmonary infiltrates involving more than half of one lung, prominent hilar or peritracheal adenopathy on CXR or CT, extreme fatigue with an inability to work, and symptoms for more than 2 months.
- May progress to extrapulmonary dissemination in about 20% of patients, producing
  - Superficial maculopapular lesions, keratotic and verrucous ulcers, subcutaneous abscesses, and/or lymphadenopathy
  - Joint and bone infections, particularly of the knees, hands, wrists, ankles, feet, pelvis, and vertebrae, which may take 2 years to manifest itself
  - Coccidioidal meningitis, which is the most severe disseminated form, with a mortality rate greater than 90% within 2 years of diagnosis

DIAGNOSIS[1,23]   Clinical suspicion is critical to early diagnosis.
- Identification of *C. immitis* spherules in sputum or other clinical specimen by culture (5–7 days) or on KOH prep or staining with calcofluor and H and E. Gram staining is not satisfactory to detect spherules.

- Immunodiffusion-tube-precipitin (IDTP) to test for *C. immitis*–specific IgM (usually positive only during first 2–3 weeks of infection)
- Immunodiffusion-complement-fixation (IDCF) to test for *C. immitis*–specific IgG (usually positive after the first month)
- ELISA (produces occasional false-positives and requires IDTP or IDCF confirmation)
- PCR (may become available in the future)
- Coccidioides skin test (positive for life, so it might reflect previous infection)

TREATMENT[1,23]   Treat for 6–9 months depending on the patient's clinical response. Relapses are common.
- Amphotericin B 0.5–1.0 mg/kg/day IV for 2 weeks (only for the most severe or life-threatening infections), then switch to one of the azoles
- Fluconazole 400 mg PO or IV Q day (for **meningitis,** give 800 mg Q day for 3 days, then 400 mg Q day)
- Itraconazole 200 mg PO or IV bid
- Voriconazole (probably effective) 200 mg PO or 3–6 mg/kg IV Q 12 hr

ISOLATION PRECAUTIONS   Use standard precautions (gloves, hand washing, and splash precautions, as needed).

A Detailed Quick Reference for

Crimean-Congo Hemorrhagic Fever

OVERVIEW Crimean-Congo hemorrhagic fever (CCHF) is caused by a virus of the *Bunyaviridae* family and produces a viral hemorrhagic fever syndrome. Ruminants and ticks are the primary reservoirs. Asymptomatic and mild infections often occur. **Mortality rates are 20–50%.** Mortality rates could be higher in an aerosol bioterrorism attack due to a higher initial viral exposure. Any outbreak of hemorrhagic fever in the United States should be highly suspect for a bioterrorism attack.

INCUBATION PERIOD AND SPREAD Incubation is most often **about 7–12 days.** CCHF is acquired by direct contact with infected animal tissues and body fluids, infected ticks, and by aerosol inhalation. **Person-to-person transmission has not been documented.** Domestic livestock (primarily ruminants) and arthropods (ticks) are the natural hosts, and natural human infection is accidental.

SYMPTOMS AND CLINICAL COURSE[1,22,23]
- Initial presentation:
  - Consists of sudden onset of fever, malaise, generalized weakness, back pain, and asthenia
  - The initial phase lasts about 2–7 days and often does not progress beyond this point.
- May progress to
  - Fulminant disease with hepatitis, jaundice, DIC, shock, extensive bleeding, and death

DIAGNOSIS[1,22,23] Diagnosis is based mostly on clinical suspicion and a history of possible exposure.
- The differential diagnosis includes typhoid fever, Rift Valley fever, rickettsial infection, leptospirosis, fulminant hepatitis, meningococcemia, and other viral hemorrhagic fevers.
- CBC usually demonstrates thrombocytopenia and leukopenia.
- Proteinuria and/or hematuria are common.
- Virus may be cultured from blood during the acute phase.
- ELISA for virus-specific IgM antibodies from blood or CSF (usually only after 5–14 days of illness)
- Antigen detection by ELISA
- In suspected cases of any hemorrhagic fever, the local department of health or the CDC should be contacted immediately to aid in the definitive diagnosis.
- Caution should be observed in handling specimens due to aerosol risk.

TREATMENT[1,22,23]
- Supportive treatment with IV fluids and colloids and management of coagulopathy have been successful.

- Ribavirin IV 30 mg/kg loading dose, then 15 mg/kg Q 6 hr for 4 days, then 7.5 mg/kg Q 8 hr for 6 additional days may be helpful.
- Interferon and convalescent human plasma may be helpful.

ISOLATION PRECAUTIONS   Use contact precautions (gloves, gown, hand washing, and splash precautions).

A Detailed Quick Reference for

Dengue Fever (Dengue Hemorrhagic Fever)

OVERVIEW   Dengue fever is caused by a virus of the Flavivirus family and produces a viral hemorrhagic fever syndrome with hepatitis, very similar to yellow fever. The attack rate is about 80% of those exposed, but asymptomatic and mild infections are the rule, especially in children. It occurs naturally in South and Central America and often produces cases in the southwestern United States and in Hawaii. Mortality rates are about 1% with good medical care and 20% without. It rarely progresses beyond the prodromal phase, making it a relatively poor choice for a biological weapon.

INCUBATION PERIOD AND SPREAD   Incubation is **3–15 days (usually 4–8 days).** **Direct person-to-person transmission has not been documented,** although blood is infectious during the initial phase when viremia is present. Mosquitoes serve as the natural reservoir and vector and may produce secondary cases following a terrorist attack.

SYMPTOMS AND CLINICAL COURSE[1,2,5,22,23]
- Initial presentation:
  - Sudden onset of flulike illness with fever, chills, malaise, arthralgias, myalgias, severe frontal headache, retro-orbital pain, generalized flushing, prominent low back pain, and dysesethesia of the skin.
  - It may also present with prostration, abdominal tenderness, nausea, vomiting, anorexia, hepatitis, and generalized flushing that progresses to a macular or scarlatiniform rash over 3–4 days (sparing palms and soles).
  - Even without progression to frank hemorrhagic fever there may be petichiae on extensor surfaces of limbs, GI and mucosal bleeding, and hemoptysis.
  - The initial (prodromal) phase lasts 2–7 days.
- May progress to
  - Dengue hemorrhagic fever (DHF) with hypotension, restlessness, diaphoresis, abdominal pain, diffuse petichiae and ecchymosis, mucosal and GI bleeding, ascites, organomegaly, cyanosis, and sudden shock.
  - CXR may show pleural effusions and/or ARDS.
  - Laboratory tests usually show thrombocytopenia, ↑ HCT, ↑ LFTs, hypoalbuminemia, and albuminuria and/or hematuria.
  - DHF lasts 7–10 days, with a mortality rate up to 80%.

DIAGNOSIS[1,2,5,22,23]   Diagnosis is based mostly on clinical suspicion and history of possible exposure.
- Virus culture from blood during the acute phase
- ELISA for virus-specific IgM antibodies from blood
- PCR (may be available from the CDC)

TREATMENT[1,2,5,22,23]
- Initiate supportive treatment with IV fluids, whole blood, and management of coagulopathy with platelets, FFP, and vitamin K.

- Use drugs dependent on hepatic metabolism with caution, and avoid the use of aspirin.
- Watch for and treat late secondary bacterial infections.

ISOLATION PRECAUTIONS   Use standard precautions (gloves, hand washing, and splash precautions, as needed).

A Detailed Quick Reference for

Domoic Acid (Amnesic Shellfish Poisoning)

OVERVIEW Domoic acid is a heat- and cold-stable, water-soluble tricarboxylic amino acid that is an analogue of glutamic acid. It is naturally produced by the algae *Nitzschia pungens*. Human intoxication generally occurs by ingestion of shellfish (primarily mussels and clams) that have fed on the algae and concentrated the toxin. Important for its use as a biological weapon is the fact that in addition to GI absorption, **it can be absorbed via mucous membranes and by inhalation of an aerosol.** Its mechanism of toxicity is presently uncertain, but it may be related to its ability to attach to glutamic acid binding sites and by changes it produces in intracellular Ca^{2+} concentrations. Clinically, it produces neurotoxicity that can lead to neuronal death, especially in the temporal lobes and hippocampus.

INCUBATION PERIOD The incubation period is **3–24 hr**, depending on the size and route of exposure. **Person-to-person transmission does not occur.**

SYMPTOMS AND CLINICAL COURSE[13,14]
- Initial presentation:
  - Consists of nausea, vomiting, diarrhea, abdominal cramping, and severe headache within the first 24 hr following intoxication. Onset may be gradual.
- Progresses to
  - Confusion, hyporeflexia, short-term memory loss, disorientation, motor weakness, and mental status varying from agitation to coma.
  - **Maximal neurologic deficits peak at about 4 hr following ingestion in mild cases, and at about 72 hr in severe intoxications.**
  - Seizures, profuse respiratory secretions, and cardiac arrhythmias may also be present.
  - GI absorption of toxin is slow, and the onset and early course following inhalation may be quicker. Improvement may take up to 12 weeks. The risk of permanent neurologic sequelae, such as memory disturbances, increases in victims who develop neurologic symptoms within 48 hr of the initial intoxication.

DIAGNOSIS[13,14] Clinical suspicion is critical.
- Mouse assay with observation for 4 hr. Call your local health department or the CDC if suspicious.

TREATMENT[13,14] No specific treatment is available. Give symptomatic and supportive care only. Use diazepam or phenobarbital to control seizures, as phenytoin (Dilantin) may be less effective in this case.

ISOLATION PRECAUTIONS Use standard precautions (gloves, hand washing, and splash precautions, as needed).

A Detailed Quick Reference for

Ebola and Marburg Viruses

OVERVIEW   Both of these viruses of the *Filoviridae* family produce similar viral hemorrhagic fever syndromes. They are among the most pathogenic viruses known, with mortality rates up to 90% (25–90% depending on viral strain) of all symptomatic cases. Ebola is more common, but little is known about the ecology of either of these viruses. Asymptomatic and mild infections are known to occur, but they are not common. The Russian biowarfare program has weaponized both viruses, and Iraq is also believed to have attempted weaponization. Any outbreak on any continent other than Africa should be highly suspect for a bioterrorism attack.

INCUBATION PERIOD AND SPREAD   Incubation for **Ebola is 2–21 days** (most often about 7 days) and **2–14 days for Marburg.** Both are spread by direct contact with infected tissues and body fluids and probably by aerosol inhalation. **Person-to-person transmission has been documented, although it is not common.** Only 3–10 Marburg virions are sufficient to produce infection.

SYMPTOMS AND CLINICAL COURSE[1,2,5,6,22,23,28]
- Initial presentation:
  - Consists of sudden onset of a flulike illness with fever, chills, headache, myalgia, generalized weakness, prostration, cough, sore throat, and conjunctivitis.
  - This stage lasts 4–7 days, and the disease often does not progress beyond this point.
- May progress to
  - Nausea, vomiting, diarrhea, abdominal pain, photophobia, maculopapular rash (around day 5), DIC, internal and external hemorrhages, multiorgan failure with jaundice and renal insufficiency, and death.

DIAGNOSIS[1,2,5,6,22,23,28]   Diagnosis is based mostly on clinical suspicion and a history of possible exposure.
- Differential diagnosis includes typhoid fever, rickettsial infection, leptospirosis, fulminant hepatitis, meningococcemia, and other viral hemorrhagic fevers.
- CBC usually demonstrates thrombocytopenia and leukopenia.
- Proteinuria and hematuria are common.
- Virus culture is positive during the acute phase.
- In suspected cases, the local department of health or the CDC should be contacted immediately to aid in the definitive diagnosis.

TREATMENT[1,2,5,6,22,23,28]   No specific treatment is available. Supportive treatment with IV fluids and colloids and management of coagulopathy with FFP and platelets have been somewhat successful. Convalescent human plasma, if available, may be helpful.

ISOLATION PRECAUTIONS   Use airborne precautions (gloves, gown, hand washing, splash precautions, and HEPA or equivalent mask). Maintain strict isolation or cohorting of patients with confirmed infection. Disinfect excreta and other contaminated materials with 10% hypochlorite solution (1 part bleach in 9 parts water).

A Detailed Quick Reference for

Encephalitis, Viral (Venezuelan, Eastern, Western, St. Louis, Japanese, and West Nile Virus)

OVERVIEW   This category includes the Alphavirus diseases Venezuelan equine encephalitis (VEE), Eastern equine encephalitis (EEE), and Western equine encephalitis
(WEE) and the Flaviviruses St. Louis encephalitis (SLE), Japanese encephalitis (JE), and
West Nile virus (WNV). All are naturally transmitted by a mosquito vector. **Except for
VEE, all produce mild or asymptomatic illness in the majority of cases, making them
unsuitable weapons.** VEE not only produces nearly 100% symptomatic infections with a
relatively high percentage of significant neurologic illness, but studies demonstrate that it
can be transmitted via the aerosol route and therefore can be effectively weaponized.
When released as an aerosol, the number of severe neurologic cases would likely be much
higher than in natural occurring cases. VEE has a mortality rate of <1%. Natural human
infection usually occurs in summer and early fall and is always preceded by equine cases in
the same region. **The lack of equine cases and/or an outbreak in winter or spring
should suggest a biological weapon attack.**

INCUBATION PERIOD AND SPREAD   Incubation is **2–6 days**. A terrorist attack can be
by aerosol release or by release of infected mosquitoes. In any outbreak, local mosquito
vectors would become infected, producing a secondary rise in the number of cases. **Direct
person-to-person transmission via the aerosol route has been suggested but has not
been proven.**

SYMPTOMS AND CLINICAL COURSE[1,2,3,5,23]   Nearly 100% of those infected will
show some symptoms of overt illness.
- Initial presentation:
  - Consists of sudden onset of spiking fevers, rigors, malaise, severe headache,
    photophobia, and myalgias in the low back and legs.
  - Nausea, vomiting, sore throat, cough, and diarrhea may quickly follow the initial
    onset.
  - The acute phase lasts 24–72 hr and may progress to full recovery in 1–2 weeks.
- May progress to
  - Severe encephalitis with meningismus, lethargy, somnolence, ataxia, confusion,
    seizures, paralysis, coma, and death, especially in children.
  - Mortality following this phase is up to 20%, and many survivors may suffer
    permanent neurologic sequelae.
  - Studies have shown that following an intentional aerosol release, there would
    likely be a much higher rate of severe encephalitis in both adults and children,
    with subsequently higher mortality and neurologic sequelae.

DIAGNOSIS[1,2,3,5,23]   Diagnosis is based mostly on clinical suspicion and history of
possible exposure.

- CBC often shows a striking leukopenia and lymphopenia.
- Abnormal lumbar puncture with high opening pressure and up to 1000 WBC/mm^3 is common.
- Serum can be used for ELISA for VEE-specific IgM, complement fixation, neutralizing antibody, and others.

EXPOSURE PROPHYLAXIS[1,2,3,5,23]

- An investigational live, attenuated VEE vaccine is available (TC-83). It requires a single 0.5 cc subcutaneous dose and may produce flulike symptoms in up to 18% of those vaccinated.
- A second investigational inactivated VEE vaccine (C-84) may be used to boost immunity in those who have already received the TC-83 vaccine. It requires a 0.5 cc subcutaneous dose every 2–4 weeks for up to 3 doses, or until an antibody response can be measured.

TREATMENT[1,2,3,5,23]   There is no specific treatment. Uncomplicated cases may be treated with PO fluids, analgesics, and antiemetics if needed. Severe cases may require anticonvulsants, intensive IV fluid support, and mechanical ventilation.

ISOLATION PRECAUTIONS   Use standard precautions (gloves, hand washing, and splash precautions). A surgical or HEPA filter (N-95 or better) mask may be helpful around coughing patients because of the uncertain risk of aerosol transmission. Because of possible transmission by the insect vector, control of mosquitoes is essential to prevent secondary cycles of infections.

A Detailed Quick Reference for

Glanders

OVERVIEW   Glanders is primarily a disease of horses, mules, and donkeys and is caused by the nonmotile, aerobic, gram-negative bacillus *Burkholderia* (formerly *Pseudomonas*) *mallei*. Under natural conditions, humans are rare incidental hosts. Aerosols accidentally released from laboratory cultures have proven to be highly infectious, and **in a bioterrorism attack, infection will undoubtedly occur by inhalation of a released aerosol**. There are several forms of disease caused by *B. mallei*: acute localized, acute pulmonary, septicemic, and chronic cutaneous. **Acute forms are almost always fatal without treatment.**

INCUBATION PERIOD AND SPREAD   By inhalation, acute glanders has an incubation period of **10–14 days,** depending on the number of organisms inhaled. The chronic form of glanders my have an incubation period of longer than 14 days. Natural cases are acquired from infected animals by contamination of broken skin, oral, nasal, or conjuctival mucosa, or by inhalation. The pulmonary form may result from inhalation or by hematogenous spread. **Direct person-to-person transmission via infected secretions is possible.**

SYMPTOMS AND CLINICAL COURSE[1,2,3,5,23,29]
- Initial presentation:
  - The pulmonary form is most likely after a bioterrorism attack. All forms may progress to the septicemic form and produce a papular or papulopustular rash that may be mistaken for smallpox.
  - **Pulmonary glanders** produces the sudden onset of fever, rigors, sweats, cough, myalgias, pleuritic chest pain, photophobia, lacrimation, diarrhea, tachycardia, cervical adenopathy, and mild splenomegaly. It rapidly progresses to bilateral, lobar or segmental pneumonia, and/or acute lung abscesses. It may occur concurrently with or progress to the septicemic form.
  - **Septicemic glanders** may produce initial symptoms similar to the pulmonary form, or it may occur primarily and progress to the pulmonary form.
  - **Acute localized glanders** produces an acute localized pyogenic infection usually of the nasal and/or conjunctival mucosa. This may present as severe conjunctivitis and/or mucopurulent, blood-streaked discharge from the nose with intranasal nodules and ulcerations.
  - **Chronic glanders** usually has a delayed onset (after aerosol release) and presents as cutaneous and intramuscular abscesses on the extremities with lymphangitis and enlarged, indurated regional lymph nodes. It may erupt into the acute septicemic form or resolve spontaneously. It rarely progresses to osteomyelitis, brain abscesses, and meningitis.

DIAGNOSIS[1,2,3,5,23,29]   Diagnosis is based mostly on clinical suspicion and history of possible exposure.
- CXR may demonstrate miliary nodules, pneumonia, and/or lung abscesses.
- Gram stain of lesion exudates may reveal small gram-negative rods.

- Blood cultures are usually negative until the patient is moribund.
- Complement fixation tests are considered positive at titers of 1:20 or higher.
- Bacteria can be grown in special culture media, but they are dangerous to laboratory workers.

EXPOSURE PROPHYLAXIS[1,3,4,23,29]   TMP 2 mg/kg–SMX 10 mg/kg PO bid may be tried. Length of prophylactic treatment is uncertain (at least 2 weeks).

TREATMENT[1,3,5,23,29]   **Any isolates should have sensitivity testing, as resistance patterns may vary. There is little information on the antibiotic effectiveness in humans, and most recommendations are based on limited data.**
- **Severe infection:**
  - Ceftazidime 2 g (peds 30–50 mg/kg up to 6 gm/day max.) IV Q 8 hr (some authorities advocate the addition of TMP 2 mg/kg–SMX 10 mg/kg IV qid) for 2 weeks, followed by TMP 2 mg/kg–SMX 10 mg/kg PO bid **or** *amoxicillin-clavulanate* 20 mg/kg PO TID **or** *sulfadiazine* 25 mg/kg PO Q 6 hr, for an additional 6 months
- **Localized infection** (including pulmonary):
  - Amoxicillin-clavulanate 20 mg/kg PO tid **or** tetracycline 13 mg/kg PO tid (not recommended for children under 8 years old or in pregnancy) **or** *sulfadiazine* 25 mg/kg PO Q 6 hr **or** TMP 2 mg/kg–SMX 10 mg/kg PO bid for 60–150 days based on clinical response. If there are clinical signs of toxicity, combine two or three of the above antibiotics for 30 days, then switch to monotherapy for the remainder of the antibiotic course.
- **Extrapulmonary suppurative infection:**
  - Use the same treatments as above for 6–12 months based on clinical response, and surgically drain all abscesses.
- Other antibiotics that may be effective include fluoroquinolones, doxycycline, and rifampin.

ISOLATION PRECAUTIONS   Use droplet precautions (gloves, gown, hand washing, splash precautions, and surgical mask). Maintain isolation or cohorting of patients with confirmed infection. Mask suspected patients in the ER and during transport.

A Detailed Quick Reference for

Hantavirus

OVERVIEW   There are several viruses included within this genus of the *Bunyaviridae* family. For the purposes of bioterrorism, only Hantavirus pulmonary syndrome (HPS) and Asian hemorrhagic fever with renal syndrome (HFRS) are important. Hantaviruses are found worldwide, and rodents are their natural hosts. HPS is caused by several different members of the *Hantavirus* genus, but all are native only to the Americas. The most important agent in North America is called Sin Nombre virus. Asymptomatic and mild infections are rare.

INCUBATION PERIOD AND SPREAD   The incubation period for **HFRS is typically about 2 weeks** (range 5–42 days). The incubation period of **HPS is uncertain, possibly 1–5 weeks**. Infection occurs by direct contact with contaminated rodent urine and/or feces, by rodent bites, and by aerosol inhalation. **Person-to-person transmission has not been documented**. Natural human infection is accidental.

SYMPTOMS AND CLINICAL COURSE OF HPS[1,3,23,30]
- Initial presentation consists of sudden onset of flulike illness with fever, chills, myalgias, headache, dizziness, dry cough, nausea, vomiting, and other gastrointestinal symptoms. Malaise, diarrhea, and lightheadedness are reported in about 50% of all patients, with less frequent reports of arthralgias, back pain, and abdominal pain. The initial prodromal phase lasts 3–5 days.
- Progresses to a respiratory syndrome with fever, cough, dyspnea, rales, tachycardia, tachypnea, and possible hypotension. This is followed by development of pulmonary edema, ARDS, and death in about 50% of patients (usually within 24–48 hr of hospitalization). This phase lasts 2–3 days in survivors, followed by recovery. **Suspect HPS in any sudden and unexplained outbreak of pulmonary edema or ARDS with fever.**

SYMPTOMS AND CLINICAL COURSE OF HFRS[1,3,23]
- Initial presentation consists of sudden onset of fever, chills, myalgias, headache, dizziness, low back pain, abdominal pain, conjunctival injection, blurred vision, erythematous rash on the trunk and face, and petechiae over the upper trunk and on the soft palate, all lasting 4–7 days.
- Progresses to sudden severe shock and death. Survivors develop 3–10 days of mucosal bleeding, oliguria or anuria, hypertension, and pneumonitis and/or pulmonary edema. This is followed by a phase of polyuria with fluid and electrolyte imbalances. Overall mortality is about 5%.

DIAGNOSIS[1,3,23,30]   Diagnosis is based mostly on clinical suspicion and a history of possible exposure.
- CBC usually demonstrates ↑HCT, ↑WBC with left shift and atypical lymphocytes, and mild thrombocytopenia.
- PTT is often prolonged. ↑Liver enzymes and creatinine are common, as is proteinuria.

- CXR is often abnormal.
- Culture of the virus is difficult.
- Immunohistochemistry testing for the virus in tissue or blood and/or PCR are available.
- Caution should be observed in handling specimens due to aerosol risk.

TREATMENT[1,3,23,30]

- Initiate supportive treatment with IV fluids, management of coagulopathy and electrolyte imbalances, mechanical ventilation in HPS, cardiac/hemodynamic support, and hemodialysis in HFRS.
- Ribavirin IV 30 mg/kg loading dose, then 15 mg/kg Q 6 hr for 4 days, then 7.5 mg/kg Q 8 hr for 6 additional days **may be effective only for HFRS (probably not effective in HPS)**.

ISOLATION PRECAUTIONS   Use standard precautions (gloves, hand washing, and splash precautions, as needed).

A Detailed Quick Reference for

Influenza

OVERVIEW   Flu is an acute respiratory illness that is one of the most common diseases to affect humans. There are two types, A and B. About 10–20% of the U.S. population will get the flu each year, with more than 20,000 deaths. Most deaths occur in debilitated or chronically ill people, especially those over 65 years of age. Occasionally, a more virulent form of flu virus will emerge. This occurred in 1918 when a "Spanish (swine) flu" pandemic killed over 20 million people worldwide. Interestingly, it tended to kill a large proportion of young, otherwise healthy victims. In 1997 a new form of avian flu (H5N1) emerged in Hong Kong. This strain appears to have an inordinately high mortality rate in humans, although it also appears to be contagious to humans only from infected birds, and not through person-to-person contact. Of great importance is that the genes that confer the higher virulence to these two strains have recently been identified, opening the door to creating a supervirulent and superdeadly influenza virus as a biological weapon.

INCUBATION PERIOD AND SPREAD   The incubation period is **1–4 days**, with contagion beginning 1 day before the onset of symptoms. **Influenza is highly contagious via inhalation** of infected droplets produced by coughing and sneezing flu victims.

SYMPTOMS AND CLINICAL COURSE[1,6,31,32]   Initial presentation consists of the sudden onset of fever, malaise and/or fatigue, sore throat, nonproductive cough, headache, nasal congestion, and myalgias. Chills also occur frequently, and nausea and vomiting can occur, especially in young children. Occasionally it may progress to an influenza pneumonia.

DIAGNOSIS[1,6,31,32]   The clinical picture is very suggestive, but it must be differentiated from the early flulike illness produced by many biological weapons.
- Several rapid influenza tests are available for use in offices and hospitals.
- Immunofluorescence for viral antigens in nasal secretions
- PCR
- Antigen capture ELISA
- Viral culture

PROPHYLAXIS[1,6,31,32]   Treat for as long as prophylaxis is necessary.
- Amantadine 200 mg PO Q day (peds 2.2–4.4 mg/kg bid, max. 75 mg bid) for at least 10 days
- Rimantadine 100 mg PO bid (peds < 10 y.o. 5 mg/kg Q24 hr, max. 150 mg/day) (elderly and adults with renal or hepatic impairment 100 mg PO Q 24 hr)
- Oseltamivir 75 mg PO Q day (peds: not recommended)
- Polyvalent vaccine

TREATMENT[1,6,31,32]   Treatment works best when started within 48 hr of onset.
- Amantadine 200 mg PO Q day (peds 2.2–4.4 mg/kg bid, max. 75 mg bid) for 1–2 days after symptoms resolve (type A influenza only)

- Rimantadine 100 mg PO bid (peds <10 y.o. 5 mg/kg Q24 hr, max. 150 mg/day) (elderly and adults with renal or hepatic impairment 100 mg PO Q 24 hr). Treat for 7 days (type A influenza only).
- Zanamivir 10 mg via nasal inhalation Q12 hr for 5 days (peds: not recommended for <7 y.o.; >7 y.o. use adult dose) (types A and B influenza)
- Oseltamivir 75 mg bid for 5 days (peds: see PDR) (type A and B influenza)

ISOLATION PRECAUTIONS   Use droplet precautions (gloves, gown, hand washing, splash precautions, or surgical mask). A HEPA mask (N-95 or better) might be necessary for genetically altered flu used in a bioterrorist attack.

A Detailed Quick Reference for

Kyasanur Forest Disease

OVERVIEW   Similar to yellow fever and Omsk hemorrhagic fever, Kyasanur Forest disease (KFD) is caused by a virus of the Flavivirus family and produces a viral hemorrhagic fever syndrome. The illness is biphasic often with late pulmonary or neurologic sequelae. The mortality rate is up to 10%.

INCUBATION PERIOD AND SPREAD   Incubation is **2–9 days**. **Direct person-to-person transmission has not been documented, but infection via exposure to contaminated body fluids and inhalation of an infectious aerosol has been documented.** Natural human infection occurs from tick bites and possibly by exposure to infected rodents.

SYMPTOMS AND CLINICAL COURSE[1,22,23]
- Initial presentation:
  - Consists of the sudden onset of flulike illness with fever, chills, headache, vomiting, severe prostration, arthralgia, myalgia, flushing of face (no rash), conjunctival suffusion, hepatosplenomegaly, petechiae, general lymphadenopathy, and relative bradycardia.
  - 40% of cases will develop hemorrhagic diathesis with predominant GI and mucosal bleeding and/or hemorrhagic pulmonary edema. Severe cases may develop renal failure.
  - **Initial phase lasts 6–11 days followed by an afebrile period of 1–3 weeks.**
- May progress to
  - Meningoencephalitis (in up to 50% of patients) with neurologic sequelae, such as delirium, convulsions, cerebellar signs, and/or coma, following the afebrile period.
  - A small proportion of patients develop bronchopneumonia.
  - Laboratory tests usually show thrombocytopenia, leukopenia, ↑HCT (due to hemoconcentration), ↑ liver enzymes, ↑BUN, and hematuria.
- A subtype of Kyasanur Forest Disease virus, called **Alkhurma virus**, produces a clinically identical initial illness except that it may also produce a measles-like rash on the hands, feet, and trunk in some patients.

DIAGNOSIS[1,22,23]   Diagnosis is based mostly on clinical suspicion and history of possible exposure.
- ELISA for virus-specific IgM antibodies from blood
- ELISA for antigen detection
- PCR from selected laboratories
- Virus culture from blood during the acute phase (requires BSL-4 laboratory)

TREATMENT[1,22,23]
- Initiate supportive treatment with IV fluids and whole blood, and management of coagulopathy with platelets, FFP, and vitamin K.
- Avoid use of aspirin and other NSAIDs due to bleeding potential.
- An inactivated tick-borne encephalitis (TBE) vaccine is available in Russia.

ISOLATION PRECAUTIONS   Use airborne and contact precautions (gloves, gown, hand washing, splash precautions, and HEPA or equivalent mask). Maintain strict isolation or cohorting of patients with confirmed infection. Disinfect excreta and other contaminated materials with 10% hypochlorite solution (1 part bleach in 9 parts water).

A Detailed Quick Reference for

Lassa Virus and the South American Viral Hemorrhagic Fevers

OVERVIEW   These viruses of the Arenavirus family all produce similar viral hemorrhagic fever syndromes. Members of this family include Lassa fever (Lassa virus), and Argentine (Junin virus), Bolivian (Machupo virus), Venezuelan (Guanarito virus), and Brazilian (Sabia virus) hemorrhagic fevers. Mortality rates are up to 30% of all symptomatic cases, depending on the virus. Asymptomatic and mild infections may be common. Mortality rates are 15–20% for Lassa virus and 15–30% for the others. One or more of these viruses have been weaponized by the Russian biowarfare program, and any outbreak should be highly suspect for a bioterrorism attack.

INCUBATION PERIOD AND SPREAD   Incubation for **Lassa is 3–16 days** (most often 7–12 days) and **5–14 days** (most often 7–12 days) **for the others.** All are contagious by direct contact with infected tissues and body fluids and by aerosol inhalation. **Person-to-person transmission has been documented**. Rodents are the natural hosts, and natural human infection is accidental.

SYMPTOMS AND CLINICAL COURSE[1,2,3,5,22,23]
- Initial presentation consists of insidious onset of fever, malaise, dizziness, myalgia, dysesthesia of the skin, oral ulcerations, cervical (Lassa virus) or general lymphadenopathy, abdominal pain, chest pain, back pain, sore throat, headache, vomiting, cough, photophobia, conjunctival injection, flushing of face and upper trunk, low urinary output, and proteinuria. Small axillary petechiae may be present. This stage lasts about 7 days and often does not progress beyond this point.
- May progress to vomiting, hypotension or postural hypotension, facial edema, pulmonary edema, vesicular and/or petecheal rash of the oropharynx, mucosal hemorrhages, and occasional occurrences of pleural effusion, ascitis, and deafness.

DIAGNOSIS[1,2,3,5,22,23]   Diagnosis is based mostly on clinical suspicion and history of possible exposure.
- Consider this diagnosis in any patients with a severe febrile illness, dizziness, and hypotension or postural hypotension, flushing of face and upper trunk, nondependent edema, petechiae (especially axillary), proteinuria, hematuria, and/or bleeding.
- Differential diagnosis includes typhoid fever, rickettsial infection, leptospirosis, fulminant hepatitis, meningococcemia, and other viral hemorrhagic fevers.
- CBC usually demonstrates thrombocytopenia and leukopenia.
- Proteinuria and/or hematuria are the rule.
- Virus culture from blood or throat swab is positive during the acute phase.
- ELISA or IFA available for specific IgM antibodies.
- In suspected cases, the local department of health or the CDC should be contacted immediately to aid in the definitive virologic diagnosis.

TREATMENT[1,2,3,5,22,23]

- Supportive treatment with IV fluids and colloids and management of coagulopathy have been somewhat successful.
- Ribavirin IV (especially if begun before day 7 of illness) 30 mg/kg loading dose, then 15 mg/kg Q 6 hr for 4 days, then 7.5 mg/kg Q 8 hr for 6 additional days
- Convalescent human plasma if begun prior to day 9 of illness

ISOLATION PRECAUTIONS   Use airborne and contact precautions (gloves, gown, hand washing, splash precautions, and HEPA or equivalent mask). Maintain isolation or cohorting of patients with confirmed infection. Disinfect excreta and other contaminated materials and surfaces with a 10% hypochlorite solution (1 part bleach in 9 parts water).

A Detailed Quick Reference for

Legionellosis

OVERVIEW   Legionellosis is produced by *Legionella pneumophila*, a gram-negative, aerobic, non-spore-forming coccobacillus. It is present in small numbers in most bodies of water, but growth and proliferation often occur in cooling towers, water distribution centers, and hot water tanks. It is chlorine tolerant and survives standard water treatment. Infection is by aerosol inhalation and aspiration of contaminated droplets. Under natural conditions, it rarely produces illness in healthy individuals, but in a bioterrorist attack, the large numbers of organisms released might overwhelm normal host defenses. It produces two syndromes, a **flulike illness without pneumonia (Pontiac fever) and a flulike illness with pneumonia (legionnaires' disease).**

INCUBATION PERIOD AND SPREAD   The incubation period is **1–2 days** for Pontiac fever and **2–10 days** for legionnaires' disease. Pontiac fever has a 90% attack rate. **Person-to-person transmission does not occur.**

SYMPTOMS AND CLINICAL COURSE[1,6,23]   The initial presentation is nearly the same for Pontiac fever and legionnaires' disease.
- Initial presentation:
  - Consists of a flulike illness with fever, chills, malaise, myalgias, headache, dry cough, dizziness, and nausea.
  - Pontiac fever does not progress further.
- Progresses to
  - Atypical pneumonia with fever, mildly productive cough, and possible mild hemoptysis, rales, and chest pain.
  - Occasional nausea, vomiting, diarrhea, and abdominal pain may occur.
  - Mortality rate of legionnaires' disease is 5–15%.
  - CXR shows diffuse, lobar, segmental, or patchy pneumonia. X-ray findings may lag behind clinical findings by several days.

DIAGNOSIS[1,6,23]
- *L. pneumophila* can be cultured on special media but takes 3–5 days to grow.
- Direct fluorescent antibody stain (sensitivity 33–70%)
- Urinary antigen testing for *Legionella* lipopolysaccharide (remains positive for weeks)
- PCR

TREATMENT[1,6,23]   Treat for14 days.
- Ciprofloxacin 400 mg (peds 10–15 mg/kg) IV drip Q8 hr or 750 mg PO Q12 hr **or**
- Levofloxacin 500 mg (peds: not approved) PO/IV drip Q24 hr **or**
- Trovafloxacin 200 mg (peds: not approved) PO/IV drip Q12 hr **or**
- Azithromycin 500 mg (peds 12 mg/kg) PO/IV Q24 hr
- TMP-SMX 160/800 IV Q8 hr or PO Q12 hr (peds 7.5–10 mg/kg IV/PO Q 8–12 hr)

- Additional antibiotics with activity against *Legionella* include doxycycline, rifampin, clarithromycin, minocycline, and tetracycline.

ISOLATION PRECAUTIONS   Use standard precautions (gloves, hand washing, and splash precautions, as needed).

A Detailed Quick Reference for

Leptospirosis

OVERVIEW   Leptospirosis is produced by *Leptospira interrogans* (and other pathogenic *Leptospira* species and serivars), which are aerobic, thin, finely coiled, gram-negative spirochetes with a flagella at each end. Amphibians, reptiles, and mammals may be carriers and excrete the bacteria in the urine. It can also be acquired by inhalation of contaminated aerosols. Infection may produce subclinical illness, mild to moderate self-limited illness (90% of all infections), or severe disease with a mortality rate of up to 40%. The overall mortality rate is 1–5% of all cases.

INCUBATION PERIOD AND SPREAD   The incubation period is **3–30 days (usually 5–14 days)**. Infection occurs by direct contact of broken skin or mucous membrane with infected animal tissues or contaminated urine, soil or water. It may also be acquired by inhalation of an infectious aerosol. It is **minimally contagious person to person, only through direct contact with infected urine, blood, or tissue.**

SYMPTOMS AND CLINICAL COURSE[1,23]
- Initial presentation:
  - Consists of sudden onset of flulike illness with remittent fever, chills or rigors, headache, myalgia, low back pain, and conjunctival injection.
  - Fewer than 50% of initial cases will also demonstrate cough, abdominal pain, nausea, vomiting, diarrhea, pharyngitis, and/or a pretibial maculopapular rash lasting 3–7 days.
  - Even without further progression, recovery may take months.
- Progresses to
  - **Weil's disease,** with high fever, liver failure with jaundice and hepatospleno-megaly, acute renal failure, aseptic meningitis, hemorrhagic pneumonitis with hemoptysis, ARDS, bleeding diathesis, cardiac arrhythmias, shock, and death. Mortality is up to 40% of patients who reach this stage.
  - Laboratory tests may show thrombocytopenia, ↑LFTs, uremia, proteinuria, and/or hematuria.

DIAGNOSIS[1,23]
- Culture on special media from blood, CSF, urine, or tissue during the initial 7–10 days can be done but is difficult and may require up to 16 weeks.
- PCR and immunohistochemical staining are best for rapid detection.
- Darkfield microscopy may demonstrate motile spirochetes.
- ELISA for *Leptospira*-specific IgM
- Microscopic agglutination test (MAT) and the indirect hemagglutination assay (IHA) are usually available from reference laboratories.

EXPOSURE PROPHYLAXIS[1,23]   Administer doxycycline 200 mg PO once a week for the duration of potential exposure period.

TREATMENT[1,23]   Treatment should be started as early as possible (**preferably prior to day 4 of the illness**) to be effective. **Treat for 7 days.**

- **Mild illness:**
  - Doxycycline 100 mg (peds 2 mg/kg) PO Q12 hr
  - Amoxicillin 875 mg (peds 20 mg/kg) PO Q 12 hr
  - Ampicillin 750 mg (peds 25 mg/kg) PO Q 6 hr
- **Severe illness:**
  - Penicillin G 2 million units (peds 25,000 U/kg) IV Q 4 hr
  - Ampicillin 1–2 g (peds 25 mg/kg) IV Q 6 hr

ISOLATION PRECAUTIONS   Use contact precautions (gloves, gown, hand washing, and splash precautions).

A Detailed Quick Reference for

Melioidosis

OVERVIEW   Melioidosis is caused by the free-living small, nonmotile, aerobic, gram-negative bacillus *Burkholderia* (formerly *Pseudomonas*) *pseudomallei*, which is found primarily in tropical Asia, growing in ponds, stagnant streams, and soil. It is rare in the United States. **In a bioterrorism attack, infection will most likely occur by inhalation of a released aerosol.** Several forms of disease are produced by *B. pseudomallei*: **acute localized, acute pulmonary, acute septicemic,** and **chronic suppurative.** There may also be subclinical infections, and recrudescent melioidosis occurring weeks to years after a primary infection. Mortality is high (up to 90%) after development of bacteremia and septic shock, but all other forms are rarely fatal. Mortality would likely be higher after a bioterrorist attack because of the significantly greater numbers of inhaled organisms than would occur in naturally acquired infections.

INCUBATION PERIOD AND SPREAD   Melioidosis has a poorly defined incubation period ranging from **2 days to years**. Natural cases are acquired from contact with contaminated surface water or soil through broken skin or by inhalation. **Direct person-to-person transmission is possible.**

SYMPTOMS AND CLINICAL COURSE[1,2,23,29]
- Initial presentation (the pulmonary form is most likely after a bioterrorism attack):
  - **Pulmonary melioidosis** produces illness ranging from mild bronchitis to severe pneumonia. Symptoms include sudden onset of high fever, chills, productive or non-productive cough, headache, myalgias, chest pain, and anorexia. It may progress to pneumonia and/or acute lung abscesses. Cutaneous abscesses may occur months later, and it may produce late chronic lung abscesses that can be mistaken for cavitary TB.
  - **Septicemic melioidosis** generally occurs in patients with preexisting immuno-deficiency or chronic illness such as diabetes or renal insufficiency. Symptoms include fever, chills, respiratory distress, headaches, diarrhea, pustules on the skin, and abscesses throughout the body. This form usually progresses rapidly to septic shock and death even with therapy. It may also progress to the pulmonary form.
  - **Acute localized melioidosis** produces an acute localized infection causing a nodule or pustule at the site of infection. It may be associated with lymphadenitis and regional adenopathy. Systemic symptoms include fever, chills, and myalgias. It may rapidly progress to the septicemic form in susceptible (immunocompromised) patients.
  - **Chronic suppurative melioidosis** usually has a delayed onset and involves infections or abscesses of bones, joints, viscera, lymphatics, skin and subcutaneous tissue, lung, brain, liver, and/or spleen. It can produce a protracted wasting illness.

DIAGNOSIS[1,2,23,29]   Diagnosis is based mostly on clinical suspicion and history of possible exposure.

- CXR may show miliary nodules, pneumonia, and/or lung abscesses or cavitary lesions.
- Gram stain of pus or lesion exudates may reveal small gram-negative rods.
- Can be cultured from blood, urine, skin lesions, and sometimes sputum, on blood and McConkey agar.

EXPOSURE PROPHYLAXIS[1,23,29] Prophylaxis is uncertain, with no human studies.
- Ciprofloxacin 500 mg (peds 10–15 mg/kg) PO bid, doxycycline 100 mg (peds 2.5 mg/kg) PO bid, or amoxicillin-clavulanate 875 mg PO bid may be tried. Length of prophylactic treatment is uncertain (at least 2 weeks).

TREATMENT[1,23,29] Treatment for 60 days or more may be required. **There is little information on the antibiotic effectiveness in humans, and most recommendations are based on limited data.**
- Ceftazidime 60 mg/kg IV or IM Q 12 hr **plus either** imipenem 500 mg IM or IV Q 8–12 hr (peds 25 mg/kg IV Q 6–8 hr depending on age) **or** amoxicillin-clavulanate 875 mg (peds 30 mg/kg) PO bid. Other drugs with some activity against melioidosis include chloramphenicol, ticarcillin, aztreonam, azlocillin, TMP-SMX, doxycycline, and the fluoroquinilones.

ISOLATION PRECAUTIONS Use contact precautions (gloves, gown, hand washing, and splash precautions).

A Detailed Quick Reference for

Nipah Virus

OVERVIEW   A member of the *Paramyxoviridae* family (related to measles and respiratory syneytial virus [RSV]), Nipah is a recently discovered virus that produces illness in pigs and humans and may also infect cats and dogs. Fruit bats are the probable reservoir. Presently, it is only known to exist in Asia. **Mortality is about 45%, with half of all survivors suffering permanent neurologic sequelae.** Virus is excreted in the urine and upper respiratory secretions of infected humans and pigs. Little is presently known about its epidemiology.

INCUBATION PERIOD AND SPREAD   The incubation period is **4–18 days**. Transmission to humans occurs by mucous membrane contact or inhalation of aerosolized upper airway secretions and/or urine from infected pigs. **No person-to-person transmission has yet been documented.**

SYMPTOMS AND CLINICAL COURSE[1,8,9,10,11,12,23]
- Initial presentation consists of sudden onset of flulike illness with fever, headache, cough, nausea, vomiting, myalgia, malaise, and drowsiness.
- Rapidly progresses to encephalitis with focal neurologic signs including segmental myoclonus, tremor, ptosis, ataxia, alteration of consciousness, seizures, pinpoint pupils, and hypotension. CSF usually demonstrates lymphocytosis and/or ↑ protein level.

DIAGNOSIS[1,8,9,10,11,12,23]
- ELISA for Nipah-specific antibodies combined with confirmation by serum neutralization test
- Immune plaque assay is a new test not yet generally available.

TREATMENT[1,11,23]
- Ribavirin IV 30 mg/kg loading dose, then 16 mg/kg Q 6 hr for 4 days, then 8 mg/kg Q 8 hr for 3 additional days **or**
- Ribavirin PO 2 g on day 1, then 1.2 g tid for 3 days, then 1.2 g bid for 2 days, then 600 mg bid for an additional 1–4 days
- Provide supportive care and mechanical ventilation if necessary.

ISOLATION PRECAUTIONS   Use droplet and contact precautions (gloves, gown, hand washing, splash precautions, and surgical mask). Maintaining isolation or cohorting of patients with confirmed infection is advisable until more is known about its contagion characteristics.

A Detailed Quick Reference for

Omsk Hemorrhagic Fever

OVERVIEW   Similar to yellow fever and Kyasanur Forest disease, Omsk hemorrhagic fever is caused by a virus of the Flavivirus family and produces a viral hemorrhagic fever syndrome, often with late pulmonary or neurologic sequelae. The mortality rate is up to 10%.

INCUBATION PERIOD AND SPREAD   Incubation is **2–9 days. Direct person-to-person transmission has not been documented**, but **infection via exposure to infected body fluids and inhalation of an infectious aerosol has been documented.** Natural human infection occurs from tick bites and exposure to infected water voles or muskrats.

SYMPTOMS AND CLINICAL COURSE[1,22,23]
- Initial presentation:
  - Consists of sudden onset of flulike illness with fever, chills, headache, severe prostration, arthralgia, myalgia, flushing of the face and trunk (no rash), conjunctival suffusion, papulovesicular eruption on the soft palate, cervical lymphadenopathy, and relative bradycardia.
  - Hemorrhagic diathesis with predominant GI and mucosal bleeding and petechiae may occur.
- May progress to
  - Pneumonia or neurologic sequelae such as delirium, convulsions, cerebellar signs, and/or coma.
  - Laboratory tests usually show thrombocytopenia, leukopenia, ↑HCT (due to hemoconcentration), hematuria, and ↑ liver enzymes.

DIAGNOSIS[1,22,23]   Diagnosis is based mostly on clinical suspicion and a history of possible exposure.
- ELISA for virus-specific IgM antibodies from blood
- ELISA for antigen detection
- PCR (may be available from the CDC and selected laboratories)
- Virus can be cultured from blood during the acute phase (requires BSL-4 laboratory).

TREATMENT[1,22,23]
- Initiate supportive treatment with IV fluids and whole blood and management of coagulopathy with platelets, FFP, and vitamin K.
- Avoid use of aspirin and other NSAIDs due to the bleeding potential.
- An inactivated TBE vaccine is available in Russia.

ISOLATION PRECAUTIONS   Use airborne and contact precautions (gloves, gown, hand washing, splash precautions, and HEPA or equivalent mask). Maintain strict isolation or cohorting of patients with confirmed infection. Disinfect excreta and other contaminated materials with 10% hypochlorite solution (1 part bleach in 9 parts water).

A Detailed Quick Reference for

Plague

OVERVIEW   Plague is an acute infection caused by *Yersinia pestis*, a nonmotile, gram-negative, anaerobic, rod-shaped bacterium. Wild rodents are the predominant natural hosts, and humans are accidental hosts. There are three forms of plague: bubonic, pneumonic, and septicemic. The most common natural form is bubonic plague, which is produced by the bite of an infected flea. Pneumonic plague can occur from progression of bubonic plague and would be the most likely expected form of the disease following aerosol release in a terrorist attack. An attack could also occur via the release of infected fleas. All forms can progress to septicemic and/or pneumonic plague.

INCUBATION PERIOD   The incubation period for bubonic plague is **2 to 10 days**, and for pneumonic plague is **1–6 days** (average 2–4 days). **Person-to-person transmission of pneumonic plague is known to occur** via airborne droplets produced by infected patients. One thousand to 1500 bacteria are sufficient to produce infection.

SYMPTOMS AND CLINICAL COURSE[1,2,3,5,6,23]
- **Bubonic plague:** Initial presentation includes one or more enlarged, tender, regional lymph nodes (buboes) often in the inguinal area, extreme malaise, headache, and high fever. There may also be tender hepatosplenomegaly and a small pustule or other skin lesion at the site of the initial fleabite (usually on the lower extremity). Mortality is about 50% if untreated. After about 3 days the bacteria enters the blood in 80% of cases, and it progresses to septicemic plague, which can also lead to pneumonic plague.
- **Pneumonic plague:** Initial presentation includes fulminant onset with high fever, chills, headache, extreme malaise, and myalgias. Within 24 hr there is often cough and hemoptysis. There may also be nausea, vomiting, and abdominal pain. It rapidly progresses to dyspnea, stridor, cyanosis, respiratory failure, and circulatory collapse. CXR will show a patchy or consolidated bronchopneumonia. Mortality is nearly 100% if untreated. **This form is the most likely presentation in a bioterrorism attack, which should be considered in any outbreak of pheumonic without pre-existing bubonic plague**.
- **Septicemic plague:** Usually concurrent with bubonic or pneumonic plague. It always precedes death.

DIAGNOSIS[1,2,3,5,6,23]   **Consider plague in any sudden increase in the number of gram-negative pneumonias.**
- Take blood cultures (3 or more sets 15–30 min apart), and warn the microbiology laboratory that you suspect plague.
- Gram stain (gram-negative rod) or Wright stain (bipolar rod that resembles a closed safety pin) of aspirate from infected bubo or peripheral blood smear can suggest the diagnosis.
- Fluorescent antibody staining of sputum, throat swabbings, lymph node aspirate, or CSF
- Cultures of sputum, lymph node aspirate, or CSF

EXPOSURE PROPHYLAXIS[1,2,3,5,6,23]   Treat for 7 days.
- Doxycycline 100 mg PO bid
- Ciprofloxacin 500 mg PO (peds 7.5–15.0 mg/kg IV) Q12 hr

TREATMENT[1,2,3,5,6,23]   **Treatment must be started within 24 hr of the onset of pneumonia to be effective. Treat for 10 days.** Do not withhold doxycycline or ciprofloxacin from children or pregnant women.
- Streptomycin 1 g IM Q12 hr (peds 15 mg/kg Q12 hr up to 1 g Q12 hr)
- Gentamicin 1.0–1.7 mg/kg Q8 hr or 5 mg/kg Q day IV or IM (peds: varies by age; see PDR)
- Doxycycline 100 mg IV Q12 hr (peds 1–2 mg/kg IV Q12 hr)
- Chloramphenicol **(add for plague meningitis)** 1 g IV Q6 hr (peds 75–100 mg/kg Q6 hr to achieve a peak serum level of 15–25 µg/ml and a trough of 5–15 µg/ml)

ISOLATION PRECAUTIONS   Use droplet precautions (gloves, gown, hand washing, splash precautions, and surgical mask). Maintain isolation or cohorting of patients with confirmed infection. Mask suspected patients in the ER and during transport.

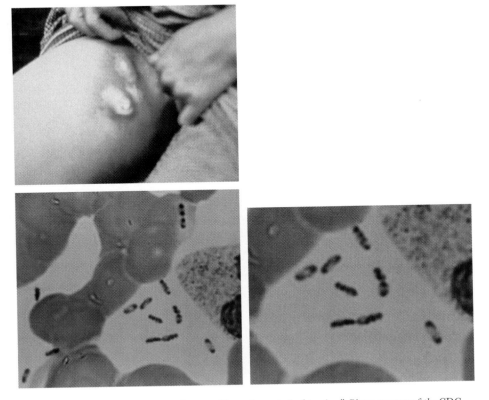

Inguinal bubos: Wright stain of blood smear. Plague bacteria "safety pins." *Photos courtesy of the CDC.*

A Detailed Quick Reference for

Psittacosis

OVERVIEW Psittiacosis is caused by the obligate intracellular pathogen *Chlamydia psittaci*. Natural hosts include, most commonly, wild and domesticated birds, but it can also infect farm animals and house pets. Human infection occurs via the respiratory route, after which it rapidly enters the bloodstream and spreads to the reticuloendothelial system. Organisms are present in the blood and sputum of victims during the first 2 weeks of illness. Subclinical infections are not uncommon. **The mortality rate is about 20%, without treatment.** Psittacosis produced by an aerosol bioterrorism attack would likely be worse than a naturally acquired infection because of the high initial bacterial exposure.

INCUBATION PERIOD AND SPREAD The incubation period is **5–15 days.** Natural transmission to humans occurs by inhalation of infected aerosol or dust and occasionally from the bite of an infected bird. **Direct person-to-person transmission is very rare but has been documented.**

SYMPTOMS AND CLINICAL COURSE[1,6,23]
- Initial presentation:
  - The onset may be gradual, consisting of fever, myalgia, malaise, and possibly chest pain, or it may be sudden, consisting of flulike illness with high fever, chills, myalgias, malaise, headache, chest pain, and crepitant rales. Hepatomegaly is common.
  - A prominent, nonproductive hacking cough usually develops within the first few days. The cough may become productive of scant mucoid and occasionally blood-tinged sputum as the illness progresses.
  - Relative bradycardia is often present.
  - Dyspnea, cervical lymphadenopathy, pharyngitis, and/or splenomegaly may also occur.
  - A pink, blanching, maculopapular rash may rarely develop (Horder's spots), which resembles the rose spots of typhoid fever.
  - CXR is abnormal in up to 90% of symptomatic patients, with findings of nodular, segmental, or lobar consolidation. Miliary, patchy, or diffuse (ground-glass) infiltrates are also common findings.
  - Less common symptoms that occur in fewer than half of all patients include nausea, vomiting, abdominal pain, constipation, epistaxis, diaphoresis, photophobia, and tinnitus.
- May progress to
  - Respiratory failure and collapse, leading to death
  - Pericarditis or "culture-negative" endocarditis
  - Hepatitis with rare jaundice
  - Anemia secondary to hemolysis, pancytopenia, and/or DIC
  - A reactive polyarticular arthritis, which may appear up to 4 weeks following the illness
  - Neurologic abnormalities including cranial nerve palsy, deafness, ataxia, confusion, meningitis, encephalitis, and seizures

DIAGNOSIS[1,6,23]   Clinical suspicion is critical to early diagnosis.
- IgM microimmunofluorescence (MIF) testing is the current recommendation, but it is imperfect and may be confounded by early antibiotic therapy.
- Culture from blood and sputum is possible, but it is difficult and dangerous for laboratory personnel.
- PCR, direct fluorescent antibody assay, and ELISA are presently still investigational.

TREATMENT[1,6,23]   Treat for 10–21 days (7–10 days after defervescence).
- Doxycycline 100 mg (peds 2.5 mg/kg) PO or IV Q12 hr
- Tetracycline 500 mg (peds 6.25–12.5 mg/kg) PO or IV qid
- Erythromycin is an alternative, but it may be less effective in severe cases.

ISOLATION PRECAUTIONS   Use droplet precautions (gloves, gown, hand washing, splash precautions, and surgical mask). Maintain isolation or cohorting of patients with confirmed infection. Mask suspected patients in the ER and during transport.

A Detailed Quick Reference for

Q Fever

OVERVIEW   Q fever is caused by the rickettsia-like, obligate intracellular pathogen *Coxiella burnetii*. Under natural conditions, it is a zoonotic infection, with sheep, cattle, and goats as its natural reservoirs. Rarely, ticks may transmit the infection to humans, rabbits, and cats. Accidental infection in humans is usually by contact with the bodily fluids of infected animals, by inhalation of contaminated dust and aerosols, and by drinking contaminated milk.

INCUBATION PERIOD AND SPREAD   The incubation period after inhalation is **10–40 days (average 20 days)**. The incubation period shortens as the number of inhaled organisms increases and may be as short as 5 days following massive exposure. **As a weapon, the organism would most likely be released as an aerosol for inhalation.** By this route, it is highly infectious, with only a single inhaled organism necessary to produce clinical infection. **Direct person-to-person transmission has not been documented.**

SYMPTOMS AND CLINICAL COURSE[1,2,3,5,23]
- Initial presentation:
    - Consists of a flulike illness with high fever, chills, malaise, fatigue, headache, anorexia, and myalgias. There is no rash.
    - Headache and fever up to 104°F (40°C) often persist as the principal symptoms.
- Progresses to
    - Atypical pneumonia in 50% of infected patients, and less commonly hepatitis.
    - Cough, chest pain, and rales may develop in 25% of infected patients after 4–5 days of illness.
    - It may rarely progress to culture-negative endocarditis, aseptic meningitis, encephalitis, and osteomyelitis. These chronic manifestations occur in 2–11% of infected, untreated patients.
    - Most commonly, the illness follows a benign, self-limited course with resolution in 1–2 weeks.
    - Death is rare even without antibiotic therapy (except endocarditis, which is usually fatal if untreated).

DIAGNOSIS[1,2,3,5,23]   Diagnosis is based mostly on clinical suspicion and a history of possible exposure. It must be differentiated from mycoplasma, legionella, chlamydia, tularemia, and plague.
- CXR often shows a patchy pneumonitis, frequently appearing worse than symptoms would suggest.
- Indirect fluorescent antibody (IFA) for detection of specific IgM antibodies is the diagnostic test of choice.
- Fourfold or greater rise seen between acute and convalescent complement-fixation antibody titers against *C. burnetii* (requires weeks to occur).
- Attempts at culture from blood, sputum, or urine are very difficult and hazardous and should not be considered.

TREATMENT[1,2,3,5,23]
- Doxycycline 100 mg (peds 2.5 mg/kg) PO Q12 hr for 5–7 days
- Tetracycline 500 mg (peds 6.25–12.5 mg/kg) PO qid for 5–7 days
- Ciprofloxacin 500 mg (peds 10–15 mg/kg) PO Q12 hr for 5–7 days
- Treatment of **Q fever endocarditis** requires **3 years** with
  - Doxycycline 100 mg (peds 2.5 mg/kg) PO Q12 hr **plus either** rifampin 600 mg (peds 10–20 mg/kg) PO Q day **or** ciprofloxacin 500 mg (peds 10–15 mg/kg) PO Q12 hr

ISOLATION PRECAUTIONS   Use standard precautions (gloves, hand washing, and splash precautions, as needed).

A Detailed Quick Reference for

Ricin and Abrin

OVERVIEW Both ricin and abrin are structurally similar, potent biological cytotoxins (lectins). Ricin is derived from the bean of the castor plant (*Rincinus communis*), which is found worldwide. Abrin is derived from the less common rosary pea (*Abrus precatorius*). Extraction of either toxin is not complicated, and instructions for preparing them can be found on the Internet. Both toxins are structurally very similar, with identical mechanisms of toxicity, and are rapidly toxic to cells by inhibition of protein synthesis. Abrin is about 75 times more toxic than ricin, by weight. In a bioterrorism attack, they can be delivered by aerosol inhalation or ingestion and are highly toxic by all routes. Individual attacks with ricin have also been documented via parenteral injection. Studies show that upon inhalation they produce a necrotizing tracheitis, bronchitis, bronchiolitis, and interstitial pneumonia. Mortality is variable, depending on the size of the exposure and the route, but would likely be high (especially following aerosol exposure), occurring 36–72 hours following a lethal dose. Other similar toxic substances include modeccin, which is derived from the African succulent *Adenia digitata*; volkensin, which is derived from the African succulent *Adenia volkensii*; and viscum albumin (mistletoe) lectin I, which is derived from certain strains of mistletoe. **Ricin is known to have been produced by Iraq and several terrorist groups.**

INCUBATION (LATENT) PERIOD The incubation period is usually **4–8 hr after inhalation and within 2 hr following ingestion. Person-to-person transmission does not occur.**

SYMPTOMS AND CLINICAL COURSE[2,3,5,33,34]
- Inhalation:
  - Initial presentation consists of fever, cough, dyspnea, chest tightness, nausea, and arthralgias.
  - Progresses to cyanosis, pulmonary edema, and ARDS.
- Ingestion:
  - Initial presentation consists of abdominal pain, nausea, vomiting, and GI hemorrhage with hematemesis and hematochezia.
  - May progress to shock and death or appear to improve. The victim may appear better for 1–5 days, then develop necrosis of the liver, spleen, and/or kidneys, and develop CNS manifestations.

DIAGNOSIS[2,3,5,33,34] Clinical suspicion is critical, and ricin intoxication should be considered in any cluster of patients with acute, unexplained, pulmonary injury or GI bleeding.
- Laboratory and radiologic findings are nonspecific, such as bilateral infiltrates on CXR, hypoxemia, and neutrophilic leukocytosis.
- ELISA testing for ricin-specific antibodies can be performed.
- PCR for castor plant or rosary pea DNA (if available) can be performed.

TREATMENT[3,5,33,34]
- Initiate symptomatic and supportive care with oxygen, IV fluids and electrolytes, and intubation with mechanical ventilation if needed.
- Perform GI decontamination with gastric lavage, magnesium citrate, and activated charcoal even after an aerosol attack because some of the toxin may be swallowed as well as inhaled.

ISOLATION PRECAUTIONS   Use standard precautions (gloves, hand washing, and splash precautions, as needed). External decontamination of victims with soap and water may be required.

A Detailed Quick Reference for

Rift Valley Fever

OVERVIEW   Rift Valley fever (RVF) is caused by a virus of the *Bunyaviridae* family and produces a viral hemorrhagic fever syndrome. Asymptomatic and mild infections occur often. Mortality rates are less than 1% but could be higher in an aerosol bioterrorism attack due to a higher initial viral exposure. Any outbreak of hemorrhagic fever in North America should be highly suspect for a bioterrorism attack. RVF also has the potential to produce significant agricultural economic damage from the loss of infected cattle, sheep, and other farm animals.

INCUBATION PERIOD AND SPREAD   Incubation is most often about **2–6 days.** RVF is contagious by direct contact with infected tissues and body fluids, by infected mosquitoes, and by aerosol inhalation. **Person-to-person transmission has not been documented.** Domestic livestock (primarily ruminants) and mosquitoes are the natural hosts and reservoir, and natural human infection is accidental.

SYMPTOMS AND CLINICAL COURSE[1,22,23]
- Initial presentation:
  - Consists of sudden onset of fever, malaise, generalized weakness, back pain, and asthenia.
  - 10% of patients with RVF develop retinitis and vasculitis, which can lead to permanent blindness.
  - The initial phase lasts about 2–7 days and often does not progress beyond this point.
- May progress to
  - Fulminant disease with hepatitis, jaundice, DIC, shock, extensive bleeding, and death.
  - A fatal encephalitis occurs rarely.

DIAGNOSIS[1,22,23]   Diagnosis is based mostly on clinical suspicion and a history of possible exposure.
- The differential diagnosis includes typhoid fever, CCHF, rickettsial infection, leptospirosis, fulminant hepatitis, meningococcemia, and other viral hemorrhagic fevers.
- CBC usually demonstrates thrombocytopenia and leukopenia.
- Proteinuria and/or hematuria are common.
- Virus can be cultured from blood during the acute phase.
- ELISA for virus-specific IgM antibodies from blood or CSF (usually only after 5–14 days of illness)
- Antigen detection by ELISA
- In suspected cases, the local department of health or the CDC should be contacted immediately to aid in the definitive diagnosis.
- Caution should be observed in handling specimens due to aerosol risk.

TREATMENT[1,22,23]

- Supportive treatment with IV fluids and colloids and management of coagulopathy have been successful.
- An investigational vaccine (MP-12) for RVF shows promise.
- Ribavirin IV 30 mg/kg loading dose, then 15 mg/kg Q 6 hr for 4 days, then 7.5 mg/kg Q 8 hr for 6 additional days may be helpful.
- Interferon and convalescent human plasma may be helpful.

ISOLATION PRECAUTIONS   Use droplet and contact precautions (gloves, gown, hand washing, splash precautions, and surgical mask). Maintain strict isolation or cohorting of patients with confirmed infection. Disinfect excreta and other contaminated materials with 10% hypochlorite solution (1 part bleach in 9 parts water).

A Detailed Quick Reference for

Rocky Mountain Spotted Fever

OVERVIEW   Rocky Mountain spotted fever (RMSF) is produced by *Rickettsia rickettsii,* an obligate intracellular, gram-negative coccobacillus. It produces an endovasculitis as its primary lesion. It is well suited as a biological weapon because it can be transmitted via inhalation of an aerosol and produces a severe illness. **Mortality is 5% even with treatment**.

INCUBATION PERIOD AND SPREAD   The incubation period is **2–14 days (usually 5–7 days).** Natural transmission is by tick bite or by direct contact with hemolymph from an infected tick (as it is being removed or crushed). **Person-to-person transmission does not occur.**

SYMPTOMS AND CLINICAL COURSE[1,3,23]
- Initial presentation:
  ○ Sudden onset of flulike illness with high fever, chills, myalgia, headache, nausea, vomiting, diarrhea, malaise, and abdominal pain and tenderness.
  ○ The classic rash appears occasionally on day 1, in fewer than 50% of patients by day 3, and in up to 91% by day 5, after the onset of fever.
  ○ The rash is typically maculopapular at onset and becomes petecheal. It begins on the wrists and ankles and spreads to the palms, soles, arms, legs, trunk, and face.
- May progress to hypotension, tachycardia, generalized edema, myocarditis with arrhythmias, arthralgias, splenomegaly, restlessness, irritability, meningismus, photophobia, lethargy, delirium, and/or coma.

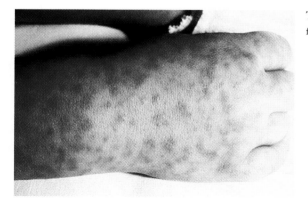

The rash of Rocky Mountain spotted fever. *Photo courtesy of the CDC.*

DIAGNOSIS[1,3,23]   Clinical suspicion is critical to early diagnosis.
- Indirect immunofluorescence assay (IFA), latex agglutination, or ELISA, for rickettsial-specific antibodies
- Dot enzyme immunoassay

TREATMENT[1,3,23]   Treat for 7 days.

- Tetracycline 500 mg (peds 6.25–12.5 mg/kg) PO qid
- Doxycycline 100 mg (peds 2.5 mg/kg) PO Q12 hr
- Chloramphenicol 12.5 mg/kg IV Q6 hr (use in pregnant women)

ISOLATION PRECAUTIONS   Use standard precautions (gloves, hand washing, and splash precautions, as needed).

A Detailed Quick Reference for

Salmonellosis (Typhoid)

OVERVIEW   Salmonellosis consists of two distinct illnesses: **typhoid** and **paratyphoid enteric fevers** produced by the serotypes *S. typhi* and *S. paratyphi*, and a **nontyphoidal gastroenteritis** produced by other serotypes such as *S. typhimurium* and *S. enteritidis*. All are gram-negative, non-spore-forming, motile, anaerobic bacilli. All serotypes can produce bacteremia with fever. Salmonella is found worldwide. An asymptomatic carrier state may exist for months after recovery from infection. There is a high degree of resistance to multiple antibiotics in many strains, and one of these most likely would be chosen for use as a weapon. Mortality of enteric fever is 10–30% mostly associated with multiple drug-resistant strains and delayed use of antibiotics.

INCUBATION PERIOD AND SPREAD   The incubation period of **enteric fever is 5–21 days,** depending on the size of the inoculum. The incubation period of **nontyphoidal gastroenteritis is 6–48 hours**. Infection occurs via ingestion of contaminated food or water or by oral-fecal contamination. **Direct person-to-person spread occurs only via direct hand-to-hand and hand-to-food contact, as well as fomites.** This can be prevented by simple hand washing with soap and water.

SYMPTOMS AND CLINICAL COURSE[1,2,6,23]
- Initial presentation:
    - **Enteric (typhoid or paratyphoid) fever** produces an acute or gradual onset of abdominal tenderness and fever. Diarrhea or constipation may precede the onset of fever by several days, along with chills, diaphoresis, headache, anorexia, cough, weakness, sore throat, dizziness, and/or myalgias. It progresses to a severe illness with bacteremia that includes high fever, headache, and weakness that may last weeks. About 30% of patients will develop a faint rose-colored maculopapular rash on the trunk (rose spots), and 5–10% will develop psychosis and confusion ("muttering delirium" and "coma vigil"). Examination often reveals hyperactive bowel sounds and hepatosplenomegaly. About 1% will suffer bowel perforation. Laboratory tests may reveal leukopenia (occasionally leukocytosis, especially in children), anemia, thrombocytopenia, ↑ LFTs, and ↑ CPK. Stool leukocytes are common.
    - **Nontyphoidal gastroenteritis** consists of the acute onset of nausea, vomiting, diarrhea, low-grade fever, chills, and abdominal cramping. Stools may be only loose and of moderate volume, or large, frequent, and watery (cholera type). Myalgia and malaise may also occur. This illness tends to be self-limited, but bacteremia occurs in 1–4% of cases (greatest in patients over 50 years old or immunocompromised).

DIAGNOSIS[1,2,6,23]   Diagnosis is based mostly on clinical suspicion and a history of possible exposure.
- Either form can be diagnosed from positive stool cultures. In enteric fever, culture is also often positive from blood (especially buffy coat), urine, bone marrow, GI secretions, and biopsy of the skin rash.

EXPOSURE PROPHYLAXIS[1,6,23]   The recommended prophylaxis is one of three vaccines:

- Live attenuated oral vaccine (Vivotif) 1 dose qod for 4 doses
- Vi capsular polysaccharide vaccine (Typhim Vi) 25 µg (0.5ml) IM
- Heat-killed whole-organism *S. typhi* vaccine 2 doses SQ 4 weeks apart (frequent side effects)

TREATMENT[1,6,23]   Treat enteric fever for 10–14 days. Relapses are common. **Supportive treatment only (no antibiotics) for nontyphoidal acute gastroenteritis.**

- Ciprofloxacin 500 mg (peds 10–15 mg/kg) PO or 400 mg IV Q 12 hr
- Ceftriaxime 1–2 g (peds 50 mg/kg) IV or IM Q 24 hr
- Imipenem 750–1000 mg IV Q 8 hr
- Amoxicillin 1g (peds 30 mg/kg) PO Q 6 hr (resistance is common)
- TMP-SMX DS (peds 10 mg/kg TMP) tid (resistance is common)

ISOLATION PRECAUTIONS   Use standard precautions (gloves, hand washing, and splash precautions, as needed).

A Detailed Quick Reference for

Saxitoxin (Paralytic Shellfish Poisoning)

OVERVIEW   Saxitoxin (and related toxins) is a heat-stable, water-soluble neurotoxin. It is produced by the algae *Alexandrium* (and other species), and human intoxication occurs by ingestion of shellfish (mussels, clams, oysters, and scallops) that have fed on the algae. Absorption of the toxin is through the GI tract or by inhalation of an aerosol. Its mechanism of toxicity is based on blocking sodium channels and preventing the propagation of action potentials within nerve and muscle cells. By weight, it is one of the most toxic substances known, being 1000 times more toxic than the nerve agent sarin.

INCUBATION (LATENT) PERIOD   The incubation period is related to the amount of toxin ingested and **ranges from 30 min to 10 hr (usually less than 2 hr). Direct person-to-person transmission does not occur.**

SYMPTOMS AND CLINICAL COURSE[2,6,35]
- Initial presentation:
  - Consists of brief nausea and vomiting, followed by paresthesias of the mouth, lips, face, and extremities.
  - Diarrhea may also be present.
- In severe intoxications, it progresses to
  - Dyspnea, dysphagia, dysarthric speech, ataxia, muscle weakness, paralysis, respiratory insufficiency or failure, heart failure, cardiac arrhythmias, and hypotension.
  - Most symptoms develop within 12 hr of the onset of illness, then begin to resolve, but they may last for several days.
  - Rhabdomyolysis may develop and should be watched for.
  - Patients who survive the first 12 hr usually survive without permanent sequelae.

DIAGNOSIS[2,6,35]   Clinical suspicion is critical.
- Mouse assay: Call your local health department or the CDC if suspicious.

TREATMENT[2,6,35]   No specific treatment is available. Give symptomatic and supportive care.
- Intubation and mechanical ventilation may be needed.
- Treat shock and heart failure with pressor agents such as dopamine, dobutamine, or norepinephrine.
- Treat arrhythmias with lidocaine.

CONTACT PRECAUTIONS   Use standard precautions (gloves, hand washing, and splash precautions, as needed).

A Detailed Quick Reference for

Shigellosis

OVERVIEW   Shigellosis or bacillary dysentery is produced by the nonmotile, gram-negative bacillus *Shigella*. There are many strains that can produce varying degrees of illness. ***Shigella dysenteriae* 1 (Shiga bacillus)** is the most pathogenic of all strains and produces illness by direct invasion of intestinal mucosa and by release of toxins. This strain is the most likely choice for a biological weapon and has an untreated mortality rate of 5–15%.

Some strains of ***E. coli***, such as the **O157:H7** strain (another potential weapon), can produce an illness that is indistinguishable from shigellosis; they have been shown to also produce Shiga toxins. Fever is a less common finding in these *E. coli* infections than with shigella. Unlike shigellosis, **antibiotic treatment of *E. coli* O157:H7 is contraindicated** because of a possible increased risk of serious complications such as hemolytic-uremic syndrome.

INCUBATION PERIOD AND SPREAD   The incubation period is **1–3 days**. Infection occurs via ingestion of contaminated food or water or by oral-fecal contamination. Fewer than 200 organisms are sufficient to produce clinical disease. **Direct person-to-person spread occurs only via direct hand-to-hand and hand-to-food contact, as well as fomites.** This can be prevented by simple hand washing with soap and water.

SYMPTOMS AND CLINICAL COURSE[1,3,23]
- Initial presentation:
  - Consists of abdominal pain, cramping, and fever, which are quickly followed by voluminous watery diarrhea.
  - Over the next 1–3 days it progresses to ↓ fever and ↓ diarrhea associated with bloody mucoid stools, urgency, and tenesmus.
  - This is followed by toxemia with high fever, abdominal tenderness (especially in the lower quadrants), hyperactive bowel sounds, and rectal ulcerations on proctoscopy.
  - Dehydration may occur at any stage. Illness can last up to 30 days (average 7 days) without treatment.

DIAGNOSIS[1,3,23]   Diagnosis is based mostly on clinical suspicion and a history of possible exposure.
- Positive stool culture during the initial days of illness (when stool is full of bacteria)
- Positive culture directly from rectal ulcer, later in illness (when stool bacteria diminish)
- Microscopy of fecal smear stained with methylene blue to show PMN leukocytes
- Direct fluorescent antibody microscopy may be helpful.
- CBC may vary from leukopenia to leukocytosis, but there is often a left shift.

TREATMENT[1,3,23]   **Drugs that reduce bowel motility must be avoided.**
- PO or IV replacement of fluid and electrolytes
- TMP-SMX DS (peds 5 mg/kg TMP) bid for 3–5 days is the drug of choice.

- Ciprofloxacin 500 mg PO bid **or** levofloxacin 500 mg PO Q day for 3–5 days
- In children, use nalidixic acid 14 mg/kg PO Q 6 hr for 5 days (instead of a quinolone)
- Azithromycin 500 mg (peds 12 mg/kg) Q 24 hr for 3–5 days in multidrug-resistant *Shigella*

ISOLATION PRECAUTIONS   Use standard precautions (gloves, hand washing, and splash precautions, as needed).

A Detailed Quick Reference for

Smallpox

OVERVIEW   Smallpox is caused by *Variola major,* an Orthopox virus officially eradicated in 1980. It is known to have been developed as a biological weapon by the Russian biowarfare program. About 20 tons of weaponized smallpox was known to be in the Russian stockpile as of 1992. It is also believed to be in the hands of Iraq and possibly some terrorist groups.

INCUBATION PERIOD AND SPREAD   The incubation period is typically **7–17 days (average 10–12 days)** but the Russian bioweapon delivered as an aerosol has an incubation period of only **3–5 days.** Contagion begins about 1 day prior to the typical rash eruption and is spread by airborne droplets, aerosols, and fomites (i.e., contaminated clothing and bedding). **It is one of the most contagious diseases known,** with only 5–10 virions sufficient to produce infection.

SYMPTOMS AND CLINICAL COURSE[2,3,5,7]
- Initial presentation (prodrome): fever (100%), malaise (100%), headache (90%), backache (90%), chills/rigors (60%), vomiting (50%), pharyngitis (15%), delirium in adults (15%), abdominal pain (13%), erythematous (measles-like) rash (10%), diarrhea (10%), seizures in children (7%)
- Clinical course:
  - Tiny red spots may appear on the tongue and palate about 24 hr before the onset of the typical skin rash. This coincides with the onset of contagiousness.
  - The typical skin rash appears 2–4 days after the initial onset of fever and usually begins on the forehead and upper arms. It spreads centrally to the trunk over 1–2 days (as opposed to chickenpox, which typically starts centrally and spreads outward).
  - Lesions are hard and feel like buckshot under the skin, are painful, and are of variable sizes but **always appear at the same stage of development** (as opposed to chickenpox lesions, which appear at different stages).
  - The rash initially appears as macules and small papules (day 1–2) → papules (day 3–4) → vesicles (day 4–6) → pustules that may be umbilicated (day 7–10) → flattening of pustules (day 11) → crusting and scabbing (day 12–14).
  - **Scabs are contagious** and usually fall off by day 21 (may last longer on palms and soles).
  - Distribution of the lesions may be **discrete** (separated lesions on face and body), **semiconfluent** (confluent lesions on face and discrete on body), or **confluent** (confluent lesions that coalesce over the face and the entire body).
  - Rarely, lesions may be flat (**flat type**) or **hemorrhagic**.
  - Mortality is dependent on type: discrete (9.3%), semiconfluent (37%), confluent (62%), flat type (95.5%), hemorrhagic (96–100%); overall mortality is 30–50%.

DIAGNOSIS[2,3,5,7]   Diagnosis is based mostly on clinical presentation. In possible or suspected cases, all specimens should be collected and processed by the local public health entity or the CDC.

- Virus isolation or electron microscopy of fluid from unroofed vesicles
- PCR
- Antibody assays

TREATMENT[2,3,5,7]   No specific treatment is suggested following onset of illness, except supportive care.
- Cidofovir has proven effective against other orthopox viruses and may also be helpful against smallpox, but it has never been tested in human smallpox and has serious side effects (renal failure).
- Best treatment is prevention by immunization with vaccinia vaccine prior to the onset of illness. Vaccinia vaccine is a live vaccine with significant inherent risks to the vaccinee and his or her close contacts.
- Once an outbreak is identified, rapid immunization of contacts and possible contacts of infected patients (ring vaccinations) or general vaccinations will probably be ordered to block the spread.

ISOLATION PRECAUTIONS   Use airborne and contact precautions (gloves, gown, hand washing, splash precautions, and HEPA filter or equivalent mask). Maintain strict isolation or cohorting of patients with confirmed infection in negative pressure room. Use extra caution when disposing of contaminated materials.

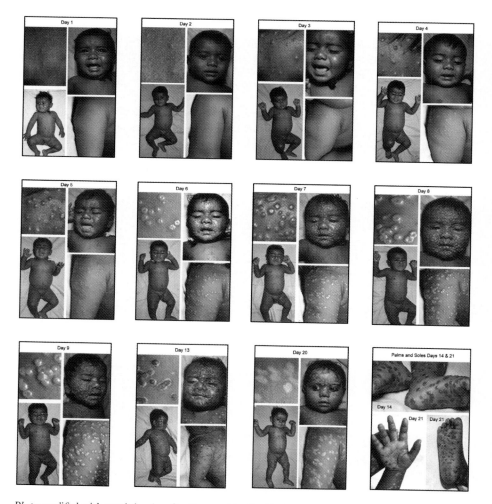

Photos modified with permission from Smallpox and Its Eradication, *1968, WHO.*

A Detailed Quick Reference for

Staphylococcal Enterotoxin B

OVERVIEW   Staphylococcal enterotoxin B (SEB) is an exotoxin produced by coagulase-positive *Staphylococcus aureus*. Under natural conditions, SEB is ingested in contaminated food and acts as an enterotoxin, producing an acute self-limited gastroenteritis with nausea, vomiting, crampy abdominal pain, and diarrhea. **When released as an aerosol (the most likely form of a bioterrorism attack), it produces an incapacitating but rarely lethal pulmonary and systemic illness.** The illness lasts for 1–2 weeks.

INCUBATION (LATENT) PERIOD   Symptoms usually begin **3–12 hours after inhalation. Person-to-person transmission does not occur.**

SYMPTOMS AND CLINICAL COURSE[2,3,5,6]
- Sudden onset of fever, chills, headache, myalgia, and nonproductive cough. Conjunctivitis may be present.
- Fevers of 103–106°F (39.5–41°C) may persist for up to 5 days with variable degrees of chills and prostration. Cough may persist for up to 4 weeks.
- Severe exposures may produce dyspnea, retrosternal chest pain, nausea, vomiting, diarrhea, dehydration, and hypotension.
- In most cases, the chest exam and x-ray are normal, but it rarely may progress to pulmonary edema and/or ARDS.

DIAGNOSIS[2,3,5,6]   Clinical suspicion is critical, and SEB intoxication should be considered in any cluster of patients with acute, unexplained pulmonary illness. It must be differentiated from respiratory infection and exposure to toxic chemicals or other toxins such as ricin.
- SEB levels in serum are transient, and it is usually gone by the time symptoms appear.
- SEB persists in urine for several hours and should be tested for as soon as possible.

TREATMENT[3,5,6]   Treatment options are limited, although most patients recover without sequelae, following only supportive care.
- Initiate symptomatic and supportive care with oxygen, IV fluids, and electrolytes.
- Intubation, mechanical ventilation, and PEEP are sometimes necessary.

ISOLATION PRECAUTIONS   Use standard precautions (gloves, hand washing, and splash precautions). External decontamination is usually not required but may be accomplished with soap and water, if needed.

A Detailed Quick Reference for

Tetrodotoxin

OVERVIEW   Tetrodotoxin is a powerful neurotoxin produced by bacteria common within several marine animals. Most natural human intoxications occur from ingesting the contaminated parts of or touching and being envenomated by tetrodotoxin-carrying marine creatures (puffer fish, California newt, Eastern salamander, parrot fish, blue-ringed octopus, starfish, angelfish, and xanthid crabs). Tetrodotoxin's mechanism of toxicity is based on blocking sodium channels, thereby preventing the propagation of action potentials within nerve cells. **In a bioterrorism attack, absorption of the toxin may occur by ingestion of tainted food or water or by inhalation of a released aerosol. Mortality may be as high as 50% even with intensive treatment.**

INCUBATION (LATENT) PERIOD   The incubation period is usually **10–45 min**, but occasionally up to 3 hr. **Person-to-person transmission does not occur.**

SYMPTOMS AND CLINICAL COURSE[3,16,17]
- Initial presentation:
  - Consists of a slight numbness of the lips and tongue, followed by progressive paresthesias of the face and extremities, chest tightness, and dizziness or a floating sensation.
  - Headache, salivation, diaphoreses, epigastric pain, nausea, vomiting, and diarrhea also occur commonly.
- May progress to
  - Diffuse weakness, unsteady gait, progressive ascending paralysis, difficulty speaking, increasing respiratory distress with dyspnea and cyanosis, and hypotension or hypertension.
  - In severe cases, there may be seizures and cardiac arrhythmias, especially bradyarrhythmias.
  - Victims who survive the first 24 hr usually recover without sequelae.

DIAGNOSIS[3,16,17]   Clinical suspicion is critical, and tetrodotoxin poisoning should be considered in any cluster of patients with unexplained oral numbness, weakness, and/or paralysis without fever.
- It must be differentiated from other conditions such Guillain-Barré syndrome (ascending paralysis), botulism (descending paralysis), shellfish paralysis, tick paralysis, myasthenia gravis, CVA, and atropine poisoning.
- Mouse assay: Call your local health department or the CDC if suspicious.
- There are no specific diagnostic tests.

TREATMENT[3,16,17]   There is no specific treatment or antidote.
- Initiate symptomatic and supportive care only with IV fluids and mechanical ventilation.
- GI decontamination with gastric lavage followed by activated charcoal may be helpful.

- Bradycardia and asystole can be treated with atropine 0.5–1.0 mg (peds 0.02 mg/kg) Q 5 min as needed.

ISOLATION PRECAUTIONS   Use standard precautions (gloves, hand washing, and splash precautions, as needed).

A Detailed Quick Reference for

Trichothecene (T-2) Mycotoxins

OVERVIEW   This class of nonvolatile toxins is produced by several filamentous fungi or common molds (*Fusarium, Mycrotecium, Trichoderma*, etc.). The most likely toxin from this class to be used as a biological weapon is T-2 mycotoxin, a yellowish, oily, heat-stable liquid that is relatively insoluble in water but highly soluble in alcohol and propylene glycol. It has been used occasionally in wars in Asia as far back as 1975 and is also known as yellow rain. In a bioterrorist attack, it would be released as an aerosol or droplets and would enter the victim by inhalation, ingestion, and direct absorption through the skin. These toxins are fast acting and potent inhibitors of protein and nucleic acid synthesis.

INCUBATION (LATENT) PERIOD   The incubation period is minutes to several hours following exposure. **Person-to-person transmission may occur via direct skin contact with residual agent on the victim.**

SYMPTOMS AND CLINICAL COURSE[2,3,5]   In a bioterrorist attack, exposure would likely occur via all routes, although in some instances, ingestion of contaminated food may occur by itself.
- Initial presentation:
    - **Skin and eyes:** Skin itching and burning pain with redness and blisters, eye pain with redness, tearing, and blurred vision
    - **Upper and lower respiratory system:** Nasal itching and pain, sneezing, epistaxis, rhinorrhea, mouth and/or throat pain, cough, dyspnea, chest pain, wheezing, hemoptysis, and arthralgias
    - **Ingestion:** Anorexia, nausea, vomiting, crampy abdominal pain, and watery and/or bloody diarrhea
- Progresses to
    - Skin necrosis and sloughing, weakness, fever, prostration, dizziness, ataxia, and loss of coordination.
    - Severe cases may demonstrate bone marrow depression with leukopenia, granulocytopenia, lymphocytosis, and hemorrhagic diathesis.
    - Fatal cases may demonstrate tachycardia, hypothermia, hypotension, and sepsis.

DIAGNOSIS[2,3,5]   Clinical suspicion is critical, and trichothecene mycotoxin intoxication should be considered in any cluster of initially afebrile patients with skin rash and blistering, eye irritation, acute GI symptoms, and unexplained upper and lower respiratory injury.
- It must be differentiated from other chemical or toxin exposures.
- An oily yellow liquid on the victim's skin or clothing is highly suggestive.
- Environmental samples, blood, and tissue can be sent for gas liquid chromatography–mass spectrometry to confirm the presence of trichothecene mycotoxins.

TREATMENT[2,3,5]   There is no specific treatment or antidote.
- Initiate symptomatic and supportive care with oxygen, IV fluids, and electrolyte replacement.

- Intubation with mechanical ventilation may become necessary.
- Conduct GI decontamination with activated charcoal.
- Flush eyes with copious amounts of water or normal saline.
- Remove patient's contaminated clothing, and decontaminate skin with soap and water.
- Environmental surfaces (but never patients) can be decontaminated with 10% hypochlorite solution (1 part bleach in 9 parts water).

ISOLATION PRECAUTIONS   Use contact precautions (gloves, gown, hand washing, and splash precautions) plus surgical mask and eye protection at initial evaluation. Avoid contact with contaminated skin or clothing. Avoid touching your own skin or eyes with gloved hands, which may have become contaminated. Use standard precautions after the patient is decontaminated.

A Detailed Quick Reference for

Tularemia

OVERVIEW Tularemia is a disease produced by *Francisella tularensis,* a small, pleo-morphic, aerobic, non-motile, gram-negative bacillus. Natural hosts include rabbits, rodents, woodchucks, muskrats, foxes, coyotes, skunks, and mink. Natural transmission is by direct contact with body fluids of infected animals, inhalation of contaminated dust, ingestion of contaminated meat, and the bites of infected arthropod vectors such as mosquitoes, ticks, and deerflies. There are multiple forms of tularemia depending on the route of infection or site of inoculation: glandular, ulceroglandular, oculoglandular, pharyngeal, typhoidal, and pneumonic (pulmonary). Only the typhoidal and pneumonic forms are significant threats from a bioterrorist attack, which would most likely occur by release of an aerosol. All forms may progress to the typhoidal form, which then often progresses to the pneumonic form. **Mortality rate is about 35% if untreated.**

INCUBATION PERIOD AND SPREAD The incubation period is **1–21 days (average 3–5 days)** following inhalation. Inhalation of only 10–50 bacteria is sufficient for infection, and the incubation period shortens as greater numbers of organisms are inhaled. **Tularemia is not directly contagious, person-to-person, although it may be transmitted by an insect vector or direct contact with body fluids.**

SYMPTOMS AND CLINICAL COURSE[1,2,3,5,36]
- Initial presentations of typhoidal and pneumonic tularemia may overlap and consist of the sudden onset of flulike illness with symptoms such as high fever, chills, cough, prostration, headache, rales, and substernal chest pain. There may or may not be superficial regional adenopathy.
- CXR may show patchy or lobar infiltrates, pleural effusions, widened mediastinum, and/or hilar adenopathy.
- Progresses to dyspnea and possible hemoptysis due to tracheitis, bronchitis, pleural effusions, and/or pneumonia. It can rarely lead to lung abscesses. **Respiratory failure may occur.** Following a bioterrorist attack with tularemia, there may also be abdominal pain, nausea, vomiting, and diarrhea due to enteric infection from swallowed organisms.
- All forms can lead to hematogenous spread, which can result in such complications as rhabdomyolysis and acute renal failure, necessitating dialysis.
- **Ulceroglandular tularemia** is the most common natural form and presents as an erythematous and tender skin papule or 1–2 cm vesiculated lesion at the site of inoculation. Over the next several days the lesion progresses to a skin ulceration with a necrotic granulomatous base or eschar surrounded by a raised, indurated, erythematous border. A flulike illness along with regional adenopathy often begins within 3 days after the skin lesion appears.

DIAGNOSIS[1,2,3,5,36] Diagnosis is based mostly on clinical suspicion and a history of possible exposure.
- The organism can usually be cultured from blood and exudates. It grows poorly, and the culture medium must contain cystine.

- Agglutination, microagglutination, and ELISA are useful, but it takes 10–14 days after the onset of symptoms for antibodies to appear.
- PCR (if available) is the recommended test for diagnosis.

EXPOSURE PROPHYLAXIS[1,3,5,36]

- Doxycycline 100 mg (peds 2.5 mg/kg) Q 12 hr for 2 weeks
- Tetracycline 500 mg (peds 6.25–12.5 mg/kg) PO qid for 2 weeks
- An investigational vaccine with limited effectiveness is available.

TREATMENT[1,3,5,36]

- Streptomycin 7.5–10.0 mg/kg (peds 15 mg/kg) Q 12 hr for 7 days
- Gentamicin 1.0–1.7 mg/kg Q8 hr or 4–7 mg/kg Q day as a single dose (peds: see PDR) for 10–14 days
- Ciprofloxacin 400 mg IV (peds 7.5–15.0 mg/kg IV) or 750 mg PO Q 12 hr for 10–14 days
- Doxycycline 100 mg (peds 2.5 mg/kg) Q 12 hr for 3–4 weeks
- Tetracycline 500 mg (peds 6.25–12.5 mg/kg) PO qid for 3–4 weeks

ISOLATION PRECAUTIONS Use standard precautions (gloves, hand washing, and splash precautions, as needed). Because of possible transmission by an insect vector, the control of ambient ticks, mosquitoes, and lice is important.

A Detailed Quick Reference for

Typhus (Epidemic, Murine, and Scrub)

OVERVIEW   Typhus consists of three separate diseases, each produced by a different rickettsial organism and each with a different mode of transmission. **Epidemic typhus** (*Rickettsia prowazekii*) is carried by lice, **murine or endemic typhus** (*R. typhi*) is carried by fleas, and **scrub typhus** (*Orienta tsutsugamushi*) is carried by larval mites (chiggers). The *Rickettsiae* are obligate intracellular, small gram-negative coccobacilli. Only epidemic and murine typhus are well suited as biological weapons, as they can be transmitted via inhalation of an aerosol and produce a severe illness. The *O. tsutsugamushi* is too fragile for effective aerosol release. **Mortality is up to 40% in epidemic typhus** (especially in victims older than 60 years), **30% in scrub typhus, and 1–4% in murine typhus**, without treatment.

INCUBATION PERIOD AND SPREAD   The incubation period is **7 days for *R. prowazekii*, 7–14 days for *R. typhi*, and 6–18 days (usually 10–12 days) for *O. tsutsugamushi*. Person-to-person transmission does not occur except via appropriate insect vectors.**

SYMPTOMS AND CLINICAL COURSE[1,5,23]
- Initial presentation:
    ○ **All three diseases produce similar prodromal symptoms** consisting of sudden onset of flulike illness with fever, chills, severe headache, and myalgia. The acute phase of the illness lasts about 2 weeks in surviving patients.
    ○ **Epidemic typhus** is usually associated with 1–3 days of malaise prior to the onset of prostration and other symptoms and may also produce a dry cough.
    ○ **Murine typhus** is often associated with nausea at onset and in 50% of cases will produce a macular, maculopapular, and/or petechial rash anywhere on the body, anytime over the course of the illness.
    ○ **Scrub typhus** is associated with a **papule at the site of inoculation that progresses to an ulceration with a black crust or eschar** that must be differentiated from cutaneous anthrax. Tender regional or general lymphadenopathy is common. Other associated symptoms at onset may include ocular pain, conjunctival injection, dry cough, and relative bradycardia.
- Progresses to macular, maculopapular, and/or petechial rash usually starting at day 5 (an axillary rash in epidemic typhus and a rash anywhere with the other two). All three may produce CNS symptoms such as confusion, delirium, stupor, apathy, nervousness, meningismus, or coma during the second week of illness. Recovery from epidemic typhus may take months.

DIAGNOSIS[1,5,23]
- PCR is the most rapid and sensitive test.
- The Weil-Felix test can be used, but sensitivity is improved when combined with an indirect microimmunofluorescent antibody test.

PROPHYLAXIS[1,5,23]   There is a formalin-inactivated vaccine only for *R. prowazekii* (epidemic typhus).

TREATMENT[1,5,23]   **Treat for 2–3 additional days after defervescence.**
- Doxycycline 100 mg (peds 2.5 mg/kg) PO Q12 hr
- Tetracycline 500 mg (peds 6.25–12.5 mg/kg) PO qid
- Chloramphenicol 12.5 mg/kg IV Q6 hr
- Fluoroquinolones such as ciprofloxacin and levofloxacin and macrolides such as azithromycin and clarithromycin may be useful but have not yet been sufficiently evaluated in typhus to recommend their use.

ISOLATION PRECAUTIONS   Use standard precautions (gloves, hand washing, and splash precautions, as needed).

A Detailed Quick Reference for

Yellow Fever

OVERVIEW   Yellow fever is caused by a virus of the Flavivirus family and may produce a viral hemorrhagic fever syndrome with hepatitis, very similar to dengue fever. Asymptomatic and mild infections are common. Yellow fever occurs naturally in South and Central America. Overall mortality is about 8% but climbs to 50% if the hemorrhagic fever develops, which occurs in only about 15% of all cases. The rest of the cases do not progress beyond the prodromal phase, making yellow fever a relatively poor choice for a biological weapon.

INCUBATION PERIOD AND SPREAD   Incubation is **3–6 days. Person-to-person transmission does not occur,** although blood is infectious during the initial phase when viremia is present. **Infection via inhalation of an aerosol has been documented.** Mosquitoes serve as the natural reservoir and vector.

SYMPTOMS AND CLINICAL COURSE[1,2,5,22,23]
- Initial presentation:
  - Consists of sudden onset of flulike illness with fever, chills, headache, malaise, myalgia, facial flushing, prominent low back pain, conjunctival injection, and relative bradycardia.
  - The initial (prodromal) phase lasts 3–4 days.
- May progress to
  - High fever, headache, lumbar pain, nausea, vomiting, abdominal pain, somnolence, weakness, and prostration
  - Hepatitis with jaundice and ascites
  - Hemorrhagic diathesis with predominant GI and mucosal bleeding, diffuse petechiae, and purpuric hemorrhages
  - Hypotension, shock, myocardial dysfunction with arrhythmias, and renal insufficiency or failure
  - Laboratory tests usually show thrombocytopenia, leukopenia, hypoalbuminemia, ↑ bilirubin (up to 10 mg/dl), ↑ LFTs, and albuminuria and/or hematuria.
  - Death usually occurs within 10 days of onset.

DIAGNOSIS[1,2,5,22,23]   Diagnosis is based mostly on clinical suspicion and a history of possible exposure.
- Virus can be cultured from blood during the acute phase.
- ELISA is available for virus-specific IgM antibodies from blood.
- PCR may be available from the CDC.

TREATMENT[1,5,22,23]
- Initiate supportive treatment with IV fluids and whole blood, and management of coagulopathy with platelets, FFP, and vitamin K.
- Use drugs dependent on hepatic metabolism with caution, and avoid the use of aspirin.

- A vaccine for yellow fever is available (contraindicated in infants under 4 months old).
- Watch for and treat late secondary bacterial infections.

ISOLATION PRECAUTIONS   Use contact precautions (gloves, gown, hand washing, splash precautions, and surgical mask).

BASIC CHEMICAL TERRORISM

What Is Chemical Terrorism?

Chemical terrorism may be defined as the intentional or threatened dissemination of a toxic chemical against a civilian population for the purpose of causing death, incapacitation, economic damage, and/or fear. Chemical weapons may be agents developed expressly as weapons of mass destruction or simply common agricultural or industrial chemicals that are also both highly toxic and readily available for intentional release.

Chemical terrorism differs from bioterrorism in several important ways. Aside from the obvious difference that chemical weapons tend to be man-made, whereas biological weapons are, or come from, living organisms, there is a much more important difference: Biological weapons, for the most part, are much more a biological insidious in their onset. Once released, days or even weeks may pass before the signs of attack begin to manifest and victims become ill, presenting to their healthcare providers, urgent care centers, and emergency rooms. Most chemical weapons, on the other hand, usually produce nearly instant and dramatic effects.

Exceptions to this difference exist in the biological toxins ricin, abrin, staphylococcal enterotoxin B, and trichothecene (T-2) mycotoxins, which act more like chemical weapons in their rapid onset and presenting symptoms. Mustard would be an example of a chemical agent that does not have a rapid onset. It requires 2–48 hours following exposure to manifest itself, but this is still a much shorter time than most biological weapons.

The fundamental purpose of using chemical weapons also differs from that of biological weapons. Because of the delay in the onset of illness, just the threat of having released biological weapons can produce profound fear and confusion in the general population and stretch medical resources to their breaking point, but it would be difficult, if not impossible, to claim the release of a chemical weapon in the absence of victims demonstrating appropriate symptoms. It is only the actual use of chemical weapons that achieves the desired result, which is always death or incapacitation, as well as fear.

The first recorded use of chemical weapons dates to 423 B.C., during the Peloponnesian War, when allies of Sparta used the smoke from burning sulfur and pitch to overpower an Athenian-held fortress. But it was not until the birth of modern organic chemistry in the late nineteenth and early twentieth centuries that chemical warfare truly came into its own. The real age of chemical warfare was ushered in by Germany in 1915 with the release of 150 tons of chlorine gas against the Allied forces at Ypres, Belgium. This attack produced no more than 800 deaths, but it initiated the hasty retreat of 15,000 panicked Allied troops. By the end World War I, both sides were employing chlorine, phosgene, sulfur mustard, and chloropicrin gases.

Since World War I, numerous devastating chemical weapons have been developed and used against both military and civilian populations. Probably one of the most terrifying and well-known chemical weapons today is the nerve agent, sarin. Often and mistakenly called a nerve gas, it is, in reality, generally released as a liquid or aerosol, and not as a gas. Sarin is so well known because of its use by Iraq against its own people and against Iran in the 1980s, and because of its release by the Aum Shinrikyo cult into the Tokyo subway in 1995, killing 12 and injuring more than 5500 victims. Sarin and other chemical weapons are believed to be in the hands of several terrorist groups around the world.

Chemical weapons can be divided into several categories, with the first major division being lethal and nonlethal (incapacitating) weapons. Table 4 lists the major weapons in these two categories. This book will deal in detail only with the lethal weapons and the

TABLE 4 **Lethal versus Incapacitating Chemical Weapons**

Lethal	Incapacitating[1]
Nerve agents (GA, GB, GD, VX, others.)	Vesicants (low doses) (mustard and lewisite)
Pulmonary agents (chlorine, phosgene, diphosgene, oxides of nitrogen, PFIB, and chloropicrin)	Urticants (low doses) (phosgene oxime)
Cyanides (blood agents) (hydrogen cyanide, cyanogens)	Hallucinogenics (LSD, cannabinoids)
Anhydrous ammonia (NH_3)	Anticholinergics (quinuclidinyl benzilate, agent 15, and belladonna)
Hydrofluoric acid (HF)	Vomiting agents (DA, DC, DM or adamsite)
Hydrogen sulfide (H_2S)	Fentanyl aerosol
Arsine	Tear gas (lacrimators) (CS, CN, and CR)
Vesicants (high doses) (mustard and lewisite)	Staphylococcal enterotoxin B[2]
Urticants (phosgene oxime)	
Ricin and abrin[2]	
T-2 mycotoxins[2]	

[1]May be lethal in large exposures and in certain patients with preexisting debilities.
[2]Considered to be biological toxins.
LSD = lysergic acid diethylamide; PFIB = perfluoroisobutylene

lacrimators (tear gas) because of the similar initial presentation of tear gas to some of the lethal agents.

Some of the industrial and agricultural chemicals that may be used as weapons are anhydrous ammonia, hydrofluoric acid, cyanides, chlorine, phosgene, chloropicrin, and hydrogen sulfide. The combustion of the ubiquitous substance Teflon produces the highly toxic pulmonary agent perfluoroisobutylene (PFIB). The accidental or intentional release of any of these chemical agents can be devastating to nearby populations, as was seen in the Bhopal, India, disaster of 1984, when the accidental release of methylisocyanate (phosgene and isocyanate) by a Union Carbide facility killed hundreds in a matter of minutes.

Physical Properties of Chemical Weapons

There are a few basic concepts that must be understood to fully comprehend how chemical weapons behave and affect their victims. Like all other substances, chemical weapons may exist as solids, liquids, or gases. Many of the weapons may exist simultaneously in more than one state. An example would be sarin, which at normal ambient temperatures is released as a liquid (large droplets or aerosol), but after release this liquid tends to

TABLE 5   **Relative Toxicities of the Nerve Agents**[37,39]

Weapon	Units	GA Tabun	GB Sarin	GD Soman	GF	VX
LD$_{50}$ (on skin) (70 kg subject)	mg	1000	1700	100	30	6
LCt$_{50}$ (in air)	mg-min/m^3	150–400	75–100	35–50	*	50
ICt$_{50}$ (in air)	mg-min/m^3	300	75	*	*	35
MCt$_{50}$ (in air)	mg-min/m^3	2–3	3	<1	<1	0.04

* Unknown

evaporate, producing a toxic vapor or gas. How much vapor is produced, and how rapidly, is a factor of each individual agent's **volatility**.

Persistence is the ability of the chemical to remain active in the environment in which it is released. This is also a factor of the agent's volatility, because the more volatile it is, the less it will persist.

The **LD$_{50}$** of a chemical weapon is the lethal dose at which 50% of those exposed may be expected to die. The LD$_{50}$ for the same chemical agent may vary according to the route of exposure, that is, respiratory, ingestion, absorption via the skin, absorption via the eyes, and so on.

To determine inhalational toxicity for chemical agents released as an aerosol, gas, or vapor, a calculation of chemical concentration (in air) over time is required and replaces the LD$_{50}$. It is expressed as **Ct$_{50}$**. The concentration of chemical in the air (C) is measured as mg/m^3, and the time (t) is measured in minutes of exposure. An exposure to a sarin aerosol at a concentration of 6 mg/m^3 over 10 min equals a Ct of 60 mg-min/m^3. The **LCt$_{50}$** for sarin, or the Ct that would be lethal to 50% of those exposed, is 100 mg-min/m^3. The Ct$_{50}$ that produces incapacitation (I) or miosis (M) in 50% of those exposed is also known for most of the nerve agents and may be expressed as **ICt$_{50}$** or **MCt$_{50}$**, respectively. These can be important values to estimate a group exposure to a nerve agent, based solely on clinical presentation (see Table 5).

The **latent period** of a chemical weapon is equivalent to the incubation period of a biological weapon and is the time from exposure to the onset of symptoms. In chemical weapons, the latent period is generally short, being only seconds to hours, depending on the route and level of exposure.

Protecting Yourself

In the event of an attack with chemical weapons, it is most likely that victims will receive their decontamination and early treatment in the field and be safe to triage and treat by the time they arrive at the treatment facility. Emergency medical technicians, first responders, and anyone else at the scene of an attack (hot zone) must wear appropriate full personal protective equipment. Rushing into the hot zone without appropriate protection risks contamination, toxicity, and death.

In some cases, patients who have not been fully decontaminated may be brought to treatment facilities and hospitals. Those patients must be fully decontaminated prior to entering the facility unless a preexisting and dedicated decontamination room with proper airflow control and drainage is present. No one should attempt to decontaminate even a partially contaminated victim unless that person is properly trained and possesses appropriate personal protective equipment.

It is extremely unlikely that any victims exposed to a chemical weapon, especially cyanide or one of the nerve agents, will be capable of transporting themselves to their health care provider or emergency facility, so the risk of a contaminated patient showing up in a waiting room is quite small. In the remote event this should happen, everyone else present should be cleared from the area. Call 911 or your local emergency number. Trained personnel will be dispatched.

The various types and levels of personal protective equipment (PPE) are the following:

- **Level A** PPE provides the highest level of protection and consists of a self-contained breathing apparatus (SCBA) and a fully encapsulated suit that is resistant to penetration by liquid and vapor. The suit is slightly pressurized to prevent entry of vapor due to the bellows action of normal movement. It has inner, chemical-resistant gloves. This level is required for work in a highly contaminated area such as a hot zone. The equipment is hot, bulky, and clumsy to work in.[37,41,42]

- **Level B** PPE provides a lower level of protection, which is adequate for most situations outside the hot zone and for completing decontamination of partially decontaminated patients. It consists of the SCBA and a nonpressurized, hooded, vapor- and liquid-resistant suit. It may also include butyl rubber gloves and boots. The equipment is hot, bulky, and clumsy to work in.[37,41,42]

- **Level C** PPE provides adequate protection when the identified agent is present in low concentrations and is known to be subject to removal from the air by a full-face, air-purifying canister equipped respirator (gas mask). The chemical-resistant clothing or suit provides some protection against skin contact with liquids and vapors. The equipment is much easier to work in than levels A and B PPE, and it does not require frequent replenishment of the air supply as does SCBA.[37,41,42]

CHEMICAL WEAPON SYNDROMIC

CROSS REFERENCES

Prominent Skin Rash, Blistering and/or Burns

Chemical Weapon	Latency	Initial Symptoms
Sulfur mustard **Nitrogen mustard** see page 136	2–48 hr 4–6 hr	Begins as a sunburn-like erythema with itching, stinging, and/or burning, and progresses to vesicles, then blisters. Ocular symptoms include pain and redness with photophobia, blepharospasm, and corneal ulcers. Respiratory symptoms include nasal, sinus, and throat burning, redness and pain, epistaxis, possible laryngitis, hoarseness, and cough, rare chemical pneumonitis, and/or pulmonary edema.
Lewisite see page 138	Minutes for pain, 2–3 hr for blisters	Immediate onset of dermal, ocular, and upper respiratory pain, followed by grayish skin patches after 5 min and erythema in 30 min. Painful blisters in 2–3 hr. Ocular symptoms include pain, blepharospasm, corneal clouding, and edema (eyes may be swollen shut). Respiratory symptoms include nasal and sinus pain & burning, epistaxis, sore throat, laryngitis, & cough that may leave progress to necrotizing tracheobronchitis with pseudomembrane formation. Occasional pneumonitis, pulmonary edema, and respiratory failure in severe cases.
Phosgene oxime see page 140	Immediate pain, rash in 30 min	Immediate onset of dermal, ocular, and upper respiratory pain, followed by patches of skin redness surrounding blanched areas in 30 seconds, progressing to wheal formation in 30 min. Ocular symptoms include intense pain, redness, tearing, blepharospasm, and lid edema, with corneal clouding, ulceration, and perforation in severe cases. Respiratory symptoms include nasal and sinus burning, sore throat, laryngitis, & cough that may progress to sloughing of airway mucosa, pneumonitis, pulmonary edema, and respiratory failure.
Anhydrous ammonia **Sulfur dioxide** **Hydrogen chloride** see page 142	Seconds to minutes	Immediate onset of skin stinging pain, redness and blistering, severe eye pain, redness, tearing, and swelling, with corneal clouding, ulceration and/or perforation, sore throat, nasal pain, sneezing, rhinorrhea, cough, chest tightness, wheezing, nausea, vomiting, tachycardia, cyanosis, and airway obstruction due to sloughed tissue, edema and bronchospasm.
Hydrogen fluoride see page 144	Seconds	Immediate onset of skin pain, redness & blistering, sore throat, nasal pain, sneezing, rhinorrhea, cough, eye pain, tearing, and redness, with corneal clouding, ulceration and/or perforation. In severe cases, there may be dyspnea, wheezing, tachycardia, cyanosis, and laryngeal swelling and laryngospasm with airway obstruction. Systemic effects include severe hypocalcemia, hypomagnesemia, and hyperkalemia.
Hydrogen sulfide see page 132	Seconds	**Low to moderate exposure**—rapid onset of skin irritation and redness, nasal irritation, sneezing and rhinorrhea, sore throat, dyspnea, painful tracheobronchitis, eye pain, tearing, photophobia, blepharospasm, blurred vision, and keratoconjunctivitis with corneal clouding. **Moderate to severe exposure**—rapid onset of gasping breaths, sweating, tachypnea, hypertension, tachycardia, flushing, headache and dizziness, rapidly followed by nausea, vomiting, confusion, agitation, seizures, cyanosis, and coma. Blistering and burns may also be noted.

Prominent Skin Rash, Blistering and/or Burns

Trichothecene (T-2) mycotoxins (biological weapon) see page 104	Minutes to hours	Skin itching and burning pain, redness, & blistering, anorexia, nausea, vomiting, crampy abdominal pain, watery and/or bloody diarrhea, arthralgias, nasal itching and pain, sneezing, epistaxis, rhinorrhea, mouth and/or throat pain, cough, dyspnea, chest pain, wheezing, and hemoptysis.

Prominent Pulmonary Symptoms

Chemical Weapon	Latency	Initial Symptoms
Pulmonary agents (phosgene, PFIB, diphosgene, chlorine, chloropircrin, oxides of nitrogen) see page 134	Minutes to hours (exertion shortens latency)	Eye pain, redness, tearing, sore throat, nasal irritation, rhinorrhea, headache, cough, and possible chest tightness &/or dyspnea. After 3 hours to days (depending on level of exposure) symptoms progress to worsening dyspnea, choking, nausea, hemoptysis, pulmonary edema, rales, cyanosis, & hypotension (from fluid loss into lungs).
Sulfur mustard **Nitrogen mustard** see page 136	2–48 hr 4–6 hr	Begins as a sunburn-like erythema with itching, stinging, and/or burning, and progresses to vesicles, then blisters. Ocular symptoms include pain and redness with photophobia, blepharospasm, and corneal ulcers. Respiratory symptoms include nasal, sinus, and throat burning, redness and pain, epistaxis, possible laryngitis, hoarseness, and cough, rare chemical pneumonitis, and/or pulmonary edema.
Lewisite see page 138	Minutes for pain, 2–3 hr for blisters	Immediate onset of dermal, ocular, and upper respiratory pain, followed by grayish skin patches after 5 min and erythema in 30 min. Painful blisters in 2–3 hr. Ocular symptoms include pain, blepharospasm, corneal clouding, and edema (eyes may be swollen shut). Respiratory symptoms include nasal and sinus pain & burning, epistaxis, sore throat, laryngitis, & cough that may progress to necrotizing tracheobronchitis with pseudomembrane formation. Occasional pneumonitis, pulmonary edema, and respiratory failure in severe cases.
Phosgene oxime see page 140	Immediate pain, rash in 30 min	Immediate onset of dermal, ocular, and upper respiratory pain, followed by patches of redness surrounding blanched areas in 30 seconds, progressing to wheal formation in 30 min. Ocular symptoms include intense pain, redness, tearing, blepharospasm, and lid edema, with corneal clouding, ulceration, and perforation in severe cases. Respiratory symptoms include nasal and sinus burning, sore throat, laryngitis, & cough that may progress to sloughing of airway mucosa, pneumonitis, pulmonary edema, and respiratory failure.
Anhydrous ammonia **Sulfur dioxide** **Hydrogen chloride** see page 142	Seconds to minutes	Rapid onset of skin stinging pain, redness and blistering, severe eye pain, redness, tearing, and swelling, with corneal clouding, ulceration and/or perforation, sore throat, nasal pain, sneezing, rhinorrhea, cough, chest tightness, wheezing, nausea, vomiting, tachycardia, cyanosis, and airway obstruction due to sloughed tissue, edema and bronchospasm.
Hydrogen fluoride see page 144	Seconds	Immediate onset of skin pain, redness, & blistering, sore throat, nasal pain, sneezing, rhinorrhea, cough, eye pain, tearing, and redness, with corneal clouding, ulceration, and/or perforation. In severe cases, there may be dyspnea, wheezing, tachycardia, cyanosis, and laryngeal swelling and laryngospasm with airway obstruction. Systemic effects include severe hypocalcemia, hypomagnesemia, and hyperkalemia.

Prominent Pulmonary Symptoms

Hydrogen sulfide see page 132	Seconds	**Low to moderate exposure**—rapid onset of skin irritation and redness, nasal irritation, sneezing, and rhinorrhea, sore throat, dyspnea, painful tracheobronchitis, eye pain, tearing, photophobia, blepharospasm, blurred vision, and keratoconjunctivitis with corneal clouding. **Moderate to severe exposure**—rapid onset of gasping breaths, sweating, tachypnea, hypertension, tachycardia, flushing, headache, and dizziness, rapidly followed by nausea, vomiting, confusion, agitation, seizures, cyanosis, and coma. Blistering and burns may also be noted.
Ricin & **abrin** (biological weapon) see page 86	4–8 hr	Fever, cough, dyspnea, chest tightness, cyanosis, abdominal pain, nausea, vomiting, GI hemorrhage with hematemesis and hematochezia. May progress to pulmonary edema, ARDS, necrosis of the liver, spleen, and/or kidneys, and shock.
Staphylococcal enterotoxin B (biological weapon) see page 101	3–12 hr	Sudden onset of fever, chills, headache, myalgia, and nonproductive cough. Severe intoxication may produce dyspnea, retrosternal chest pain, nausea, vomiting, diarrhea, dehydration, and hypotension. May progress to pulmonary edema and/or ARDS.
Trichothecene (T-2) mycotoxins (biological weapon) see page 104	Minutes to hours	Skin itching, pain, redness, & blistering, anorexia, nausea, vomiting, crampy abdominal pain, watery and/or bloody diarrhea, arthralgias, nasal itching and pain, sneezing, epistaxis, rhinorrhea, mouth and/or throat pain, cough, dyspnea, chest pain, wheezing, and hemoptysis.

ARDS = acute respiratory distress syndrome; GI = gastrointestinal; PFIB = perfluoroisobutylene

Seizures and/or Sudden Coma

Chemical Weapon	Latency	Initial Symptoms
Nerve agents (tabun, soman, sarin, VX) see page 128	Seconds to minutes (hr by dermal route)	**Small inhaled exposure**—miosis, blurry and/or dim vision, rhinorrhea, dsypnea, and/or chest tightness. **Small dermal exposure**—localized sweating and muscle fasciculations, nausea, vomiting, and diarrhea. Possible miosis. **Large exposure by any route**—sudden loss of consciousness and generalized seizures followed by apnea, flaccid paralysis, miosis, lacrimation, diarrhea, urination, copious oral, nasal, and respiratory secretions, and sweating.
Blood agents (hydrogen cyanide, cyanogens) see page 130	Seconds to minutes	**Mild to moderate exposure**—10–15 seconds of gasping breaths, tachypnea, hypertension, tachycardia, flushing, giddiness, sweating, headache, and dizziness, rapidly followed by nausea, vomiting, confusion, agitation, and heart palpitations. **Severe exposure**—10–15 seconds of gasping breaths and tachypnea, hypertension, tachycardia, flushing, sweating, headache and dizziness, rapidly followed by coma, apnea, seizures, shock, and bradycardia or other arrhythmias. Death occurs in 6–8 min from respiratory arrest.
Hydrogen sulfide see page 132	Seconds	**Low to moderate exposure**—rapid onset of skin irritation and redness, nasal irritation, sneezing and rhinorrhea, sore throat, dyspnea, painful tracheobronchitis, eye pain, tearing, photophobia, blepharospasm, blurred vision, and keratoconjunctivitis with corneal clouding. **Moderate to high exposure**—rapid onset of gasping breaths, sweating, tachypnea, hypertension, tachycardia, flushing, headache and dizziness, rapidly followed by nausea, vomiting, confusion, agitation, cyanosis, and coma. Skin, ocular and respiratory irritation and pain is common. **Severe exposure**—immediate onset of 3–4 gasping breaths followed by apnea, seizures, sudden collapse, and coma, with death in 6–8 minutes from respiratory arrest. Dermal irritation, blistering, and/or burns may also be noted.

Acute Hemolytic Anemia

Chemical Weapon	Latency	Initial Symptoms
Arsine see page 146	2–24 hr	Nausea, vomiting, crampy abdominal pain, malaise, dizziness, headache, dyspnea, and occasionally paresthesias and delirium. Red staining of conjunctiva may be an early sign. Hemolysis begins in 2–24 hr and may produce dyspnea, hypotension, hyperkalemia (with peaked T waves and QRS widening on EKG), hypocalcemia, hemoglobinuria, and acute renal failure.

EKG = electrocardiogram; QRS = TK

INDIVIDUAL CHEMICAL WEAPON DETAILED

QUICK REFERENCES

A Detailed Quick Reference for

Nerve Agents

OVERVIEW[37,39,40]   This group consists of the highly toxic organophosphates tabun (GA), sarin (GB), soman (GD), cyclosarin (GF), VX, VE, VG, and VM. The V and G agents differ in that the V agents are about 10 times more toxic and are less volatile than the G agents. This reduction in volatility means the G agents produce more toxic vapor but the V agents persist longer on clothing and surfaces after release. All nerve agents produce their toxicity by inactivation of the enzyme acetylcholinesterase (AChE). This enzyme is responsible for the breakdown of the important neurotransmitter acetylcholine (ACh). In the absence of active AChE, there is an accumulation of ACh at nerve endings, producing the hyperexcitability of the nervous system that is the hallmark of the clinically observed effects of these agents. In a bioterrorist attack, these agents would likely be released as aerosol droplets for inhalation and dermal absorption. Any residual agent left on surfaces that may come in contact with bare skin is also highly toxic. Exposure to no more than a pinhead-sized drop of VX is lethal. When irreversible binding to the AChE or aging of the agent occurs, 2-PAMCl is no longer an effective antidote. The aging time varies with each agent: GA (14 hr), GB (3–5 hr), GD (2–6 min), VX (48 hr).[38]

LATENT PERIOD   The latent period is seconds to minutes via inhalation and minutes to hours via dermal absorption (up to 18 hr for GB). Symptoms may still occur after decontamination of the skin due to prior absorption and continued transit of the agent through the dermis.

SYMPTOMS AND CLINICAL COURSE[3,37,38,39,40]
- Initial presentation depends on dose and route of exposure.
    - **Small inhalational exposure:** miosis, blurry and/or dim vision, rhinorrhea, dyspnea, and/or chest tightness. Wheezing may also be present.
    - **Small dermal exposure:** localized sweating and muscle fasciculations, nausea, vomiting, and diarrhea. Miosis may also be present in medium dermal exposures.
    - **Large inhalational exposure:** sudden loss of consciousness and generalized seizures followed by apnea, flaccid paralysis, miosis, lacrimation, diarrhea, urination, copious oral, nasal, and respiratory secretions, and sweating.
    - **Large dermal exposure:** presentation same as large inhalational exposure, but onset may be delayed by up to 30 minutes following exposure.

DIAGNOSIS[3,37,39,40]   Clinical presentation of patients with gasping, miosis, copious secretions, sweating, and generalized twitching or fasciculations is very suggestive of nerve agent exposure.
- Reduction of RBC-cholinesterase activity is suggestive of nerve agent intoxication, but normal RBC-ChE activity does not rule it out.

TREATMENT[3,37,38,39,40]
- Administer atropine 2–6 mg (peds 0.02 mg/kg) IM or IV plus pralidoxime Cl (2-PAMCl) 600–2000 mg (peds 20 mg/kg) IM or IV (military Mark 1 kits contain atropine 2 mg and 2-PAMCl 600 mg in separate autoinjectors). The initial dose (or

number of Mark I kits administered) should be based on estimated exposure and severity of presenting symptoms.

- Repeat atropine 2–4 mg and 2-PAMCl 600–1000 mg (1 Mark I kit) Q 2–5 min as needed.
- Administer diazepam 10 mg (peds 0.1–0.3 mg/kg) IVP over 2–3 min as needed for seizures.
- Administer supportive care with IV fluids, cardiac monitor, and mechanical ventilation as necessary.
- Remove the patient's clothing and any residual agent from the skin using soap and water or 1 part bleach (hypochlorite) in 9 parts water.

ISOLATION PRECAUTIONS   Isolation precautions depend on the level of patient contamination. Fully decontaminated patients require only standard precautions (gloves, hand washing, and splash precautions, as needed). Patients who may be partially contaminated (still wearing contaminated clothing or demonstrating obvious residual liquid agent) require the use of level C protection and butyl rubber gloves until fully decontaminated.

A Detailed Quick Reference for

Cyanides (Blood Agents)

OVERVIEW   Cyanide comes in four forms that may serve as chemical weapons. These are hydrogen cyanide (HCN), cyanogen chloride (CNCl), cyanogen bromide (CNBr), and cyanogen iodide (CNI). All forms may be released as a liquid, aerosol, or gas for inhalation; they may also be ingested or absorbed through the eyes and skin. Cyanide is rapidly lethal when used in enclosed areas, but its effectiveness out of doors is limited by its volatility, rapid dispersion, and relatively high concentrations required (LCt_{50}). The victims of cyanide toxicity generally either rapidly die or fully recover.

Through its binding to ferric iron in the mitochondrial cytochrome a_3, cyanide blocks the cellular energy transport (cytochrome) system and prevents the use of oxygen as an electron receptor, producing cellular anoxia. Victim death occurs due to loss of central respiratory drive, which results in apnea. Contrary to what is popularly believed from television and films, the effects of cyanide are not irreversibly fatal, and victims may be successfully resuscitated by proper circulatory and respiratory support until the antidote can be administered.

Cyanide has many industrial uses and may be produced by the combustion of many plastics.

LATENT PERIOD   The latent period is 10–15 seconds up to several minutes (depending on level of exposure) via inhalation and ingestion.

SYMPTOMS AND CLINICAL COURSE[3,37]
- Initial presentation:
  - **Mild to moderate exposure:** 10–15 seconds of gasping breaths and tachypnea, hypertension, tachycardia, flushing, giddiness, sweating, headache, and dizziness, rapidly followed by nausea, vomiting, confusion, agitation, and heart palpitations.
  - **Severe exposure:** 10–15 seconds of gasping breaths and tachypnea, hypertension, tachycardia, flushing, sweating, headache, and dizziness, rapidly followed by coma, apnea, seizures, shock, and bradycardia or other arrhythmias.
  - If untreated, death follows in 6–8 min from respiratory arrest.
  - Cyanogen chloride is a chlorine-like irritant and may also produce lacrimation, rhinorrhea, and irritation of the upper and lower respiratory system.
  - Cyanosis is an infrequent and very late finding in cyanide poisoning, and the skin may actually be cherry red initially.

DIAGNOSIS[3,37]
- The initial presentation of cyanide poisoning can be differentiated from nerve agent intoxication by the lack of copious oral and nasal secretions and miosis, although this may be complicated by the lacrimation and airway secretions induced by cyanogen chloride.
- Metabolic lactic acidosis is usually present and produces an unusually high anion gap.
- Elevated blood cyanide concentration is noted.
- Venous blood generally will appear unusually red and well oxygenated.

TREATMENT[3,37]

- Supportive care with 100% oxygen, CPR, and respiratory support as needed with intubation and mechanical ventilation
- Amyl nitrite: 1 ampule crushed and inhaled over 30 seconds. Repeat Q 3 min until IV access is achieved and sodium nitrite can be administered.
- Sodium nitrite: 300 mg (10 ml of a 3% solution) slow IVP over no less than 5 min. For pediatric patients, give 0.15–0.33 ml/kg of a 3% solution (up to 10 ml) slow IVP over no less than 5 min. Be certain to calculate peds dose correctly as overdose can be fatal.
- Sodium thiosulfate: 12.5 g (peds 1.65 mL/kg of a 25% solution) IV over 10 min.
- Repeat half the doses of sodium nitrite and sodium thiosulfate in 30 min if response is inadequate.
- Treat acidosis if necessary with sodium bicarbonate 1–2 mEq/kg IV.

ISOLATION PRECAUTIONS   Decontamination is usually not needed. Remove any wet patient clothing with caution, as cyanide dissolves easily in water. Use standard precautions (gloves, hand washing, and splash precautions, as needed).

A Detailed Quick Reference for

Hydrogen Sulfide

OVERVIEW[38,42,43] Hydrogen sulfide (HS) is a colorless, heavier than air, extremely toxic gas that produces the well-known rotten-egg odor. Exposure occurs by inhalation of the gas and absorption through the lungs. An air concentration of only 100 ppm may be lethal. Like cyanide, it blocks the cellular energy transport (cytochrome) system and prevents the use of oxygen as an electron receptor, producing cellular anoxia. Death occurs due to loss of central respiratory drive, which results in apnea, but victims may be successfully resuscitated by proper circulatory and respiratory support. HS differs from cyanide in that it also produces direct irritation of skin, eyes, and mucous membranes. It has some industrial uses.

LATENT PERIOD Immediate onset is noted for skin, eye, and mucosal irritation, and cyanide-like effect. Pulmonary effects may not become apparent for up to 72 hr.

SYMPTOMS AND CLINICAL COURSE[38,42,43]
- Initial presentation:
  - **Low to moderate exposure:** skin irritation and erythema, nasal pain, sneezing, rhinorrhea, sore throat, cough, dyspnea, painful tracheobronchitis with bronchial and/or pulmonary hemorrhage and hemoptysis, eye pain, lacrimation, photophobia, blepharospasm, blurred vision, and keratoconjunctivitis with corneal clouding. Rarely, late pneumonitis or pulmonary edema can develop, which takes up to 72 hr to manifest.
  - **Moderate to high exposure:** rapid onset of gasping breaths, tachypnea, hypertension, tachycardia, flushing, sweating, headache, and dizziness, rapidly followed by nausea, vomiting, confusion, agitation, cyanosis, and finally coma.
  - **Severe exposure:** immediate onset of several gasping breaths followed by apnea, seizures, sudden collapse, and coma. If untreated, death follows in 6–8 min from respiratory arrest. Dermal irritation, blistering, and/or burns may also be noted.

DIAGNOSIS[3,37] There is no specific diagnostic test.
- The initial presentation of hydrogen sulfide poisoning can be differentiated from nerve agent intoxication by the lack of copious oral and nasal secretions and miosis.
- A history of a rotten egg–like odor may help to differentiate it from cyanide.
- Metabolic lactic acidosis is usually present and produces an unusually high anion gap.

TREATMENT[3,42]
- Supportive care with 100% oxygen, CPR, and respiratory support as needed, with intubation and mechanical ventilation, are the mainstays of therapy.
- Amyl nitrite: 1 ampule crushed and inhaled over 30 seconds. Repeat Q 3 min until IV access is achieved and sodium nitrite can be administered.
- Sodium nitrite: 300 mg (10 ml of a 3% solution) slow IVP over no less than 5 min. For pediatric patients, give 0.15–0.33 ml/kg of a 3% solution (up to 10 ml) slow IVP over no less than 5 min. Be certain to calculate peds dose correctly as overdose can be fatal. **(The effectiveness of nitrites is anecdotal, unproven, and controversial.)**

- Sodium thiosulfate is not effective and should not be used.
- Treat acidosis if necessary with sodium bicarbonate 1–2 mEq/kg IV.
- Control bronchospasm, if present, with theophylline and albuterol.
- Treat chemical burns as any thermal burns would be treated.

ISOLATION PRECAUTIONS Decontamination is usually not needed. Remove any wet patient clothing with caution, as hydrogen sulfide dissolves easily in water. Use standard precautions (gloves, hand washing, and splash precautions, as needed).

A Detailed Quick Reference for

Pulmonary Agents

OVERVIEW[3,37,42]   Pulmonary agents (chlorine, phosgene, diphosgene, nitrogen oxides, PFIB, and chloropicrin) are all liquids and gases, but they exert their major toxicity by inhalation as gases. They enter the lung and disrupt the alveolar-capillary membranes, reducing oxygen exchange, and allowing leakage of fluid into the interstitial tissues and alveoli. These agents have some differing physical properties and frequently produce other peripheral effects. **Phosgene** and differing **diphosgene** are colorless, volatile liquids that produce a heavier than air vapor with the odor of fresh mown hay. **Chlorine** is an extremely irritating greenish yellow, heavier than air gas, with an acrid odor. **Nitrogen oxides** are colorless liquids that produce an irritating vapor. **Chloropicrin**, an agricultural biocide, is an oily, colorless to light green liquid with an intense odor. It is extremely irritating to any body surface it contacts, and it degrades to phosgene and other toxic substances. It produces lung damage at an air concentration of only 20 ppm. **PFIB** (perfluoroisobutylene) is a combustion product of Teflon and other plastics and is 10 times more toxic than phosgene. All have important agricultural and industrial uses.

LATENT PERIOD   The latent period ranges from minutes to hours, depending on the agent and the level of exposure (occasionally days). Exertion tends to shorten the latent period.

SYMPTOMS AND CLINICAL COURSE[3,37,42]
- Initial presentation:
    - Based on upper airway, ocular, and mucous membrane irritation, and consists of conjunctival pain and redness, lacrimation, sore throat, nasal irritation, rhinorrhea, headache, and coughing. Dyspnea and/or chest tightness may also present at this stage after large exposures.
    - After a latency period of about 3 hr to days (depending on the level of exposure), these symptoms may progress to progressively worsening dyspnea, choking, nausea, hemoptysis, pulmonary edema, hemoconcentration (as fluid flows into the lungs), hypotension, and fine to coarse rales. Cyanosis may also be present. Rapid progression to hypoxia and hypotension (within 4 hr) carries a poor prognosis.

DIAGNOSIS[3,37]
- History of exposure to an irritating gas
- Elevated HCT due to hemoconcentration
- Reduced PaO_2 on ABG
- CXR may initially demonstrate hyperinflation followed by noncardiogenic pulmonary edema (findings may lag behind clinical symptoms by days).

TREATMENT[3,37]   There is no specific treatment or antidote.
- Initiate enforced rest and oxygen therapy.
- Control hypotension with administration of IV colloids and/or crystalloids.
- Control airway and manage airway secretions.

- Control bronchospasm, if present, with theophylline, albuterol, and IV steroids.
- Provide intubation, mechanical ventilation, and PEEP as necessary.

ISOLATION PRECAUTIONS Decontamination is usually not needed. Remove any contaminated clothing (this should only be a problem with chloropicrin). Use standard precautions (gloves, hand washing, and splash precautions, as needed).

A Detailed Quick Reference for

Mustard

OVERVIEW[3,37,38]   Sulfur mustard and nitrogen mustard are vesicants or blister agents first developed during World War I. Mustard is an oily yellowish to brown liquid with the taste of garlic and the odor of mustard. In a terrorist attack, it would likely be released as an aerosol or droplets, with toxicity by inhalation and absorption through the skin, eyes, and mucous membranes. The LD_{50} is 100 mg/kg, and 1 tsp (5 cc) is about 7000 mg, a quantity sufficient to cover about 25% of the total body surface. Tissue damage occurs very quickly after contact, but symptoms typically take hours to appear. Mustard readily penetrates thin clothing, and thin, moist skin is most susceptible to its toxic effects. A delayed onset of symptoms after exposure helps differentiate mustard from lewisite. Because of this delayed onset, many victims will not present for medical care until hours after exposure and may require decontamination.

LATENT PERIOD   The latent period is 2–48 hr after exposure for sulfur mustard and 4–6 hr for nitrogen mustard.

SYMPTOMS AND CLINICAL COURSE[3,37,42]   More ocular and respiratory lesions than skin lesions would be expected in a warm climate than in cold due to an increase in vaporization.
- Initial presentation: The onset of symptoms tends to be earlier for nitrogen mustard.
    - 2–24 hr after exposure the skin develops a mild sunburn-like erythema with itching, burning, and/or stinging. This progresses to small vesicles that may coalesce to form large, yellowish, thin-walled bullae over the areas of erythema.
    - Ocular symptoms include irritation and redness that progress to conjunctivitis with lacrimation, pain, photophobia, blepharospasm, and corneal ulceration. These effects may persist for up to 10 days and may begin as soon as 20 min after exposure to nitrogen mustard.
    - Respiratory symptoms include burning and irritation of nasal mucosa and sinuses, epistaxis, and sore throat. In moderate exposures, this also includes laryngitis, hoarseness, and dry cough. In severe exposures, there may be necrosis and sloughing of the airway mucosa, and rarely pulmonary edema and a clinical picture similar to that of the pulmonary agents.
    - Nausea and vomiting are not uncommon.
    - Late effects may include bone marrow suppression and pancytopenia beginning 3–5 days after exposure.
    - Death often occurs between days 5 and 10 after exposure due to pulmonary insufficiency and infection resulting from a compromised immune system.

DIAGNOSIS[3,37]
- History of exposure to an irritating gas and clinical presentation
- CBC may show initial leukocytosis on day 1; if the exposure was large, there may be a precipitous drop in leukocytes beginning day 3–5 that represents bone marrow injury.
- Urinary thiodiglycol (a mustard metabolite) can be detected for up to 1 week.

- CXR may initially be normal but progress to findings of chemical pneumonitis in the first 2–3 days.

TREATMENT[3,37,38,42]   There is no specific treatment or antidote.
- Patient's skin must be decontaminated as soon as possible with 1 part bleach in 9 parts water, or soap and water. This should be done prior to arrival at the treatment facility.
- Treat blisters and skin lesions the same as thermal burns. Blister fluid does not contain mustard, and the blisters may be safely unroofed.
- Control pain with liberal systemic analgesics.
- Control bronchospasm, if present, with theophylline, albuterol, and IV steroids.
- Provide oxygen, intubation, mechanical ventilation, and PEEP or CPAP as necessary. If intubation seems likely, it should be performed early before laryngeal spasm and edema make it too difficult or impossible.
- Sodium thiosulfate (50 ml of a 25% solution IV over 10 min) and N-acetylcysteine (140 mg/kg PO followed by 40 mg/kg PO Q 4 hrs for 17 doses) may be useful before or immediately following exposure, but they have not been shown to have any beneficial effect after 20 min following exposure.

ISOLATION PRECAUTIONS   Victims should be decontaminated prior to arrival at the treatment facility. Use standard precautions (gloves, hand washing, and splash precautions, as needed).

A Detailed Quick Reference for

Lewisite

OVERVIEW[3,37,38]   Lewisite is a vesicant or blister agent whose use dates back to just
after World War I. It is an oily, colorless liquid that is more volatile than mustard. In a
terrorist attack, it would likely be released as an aerosol or droplets, and toxicity occurs by
inhalation and absorption through the skin, eyes, and mucous membranes. Exposure to
lewisite vapor or liquid produces the immediate onset of pain, which differs from
mustard's long delay of hours before the onset of pain and other symptoms. The LD_{50}
of liquid lewisite on the skin is about 2800 mg.

LATENT PERIOD   Pain occurs within minutes and blisters within 2–3 hr.

SYMPTOMS AND CLINICAL COURSE[3,37]
- Initial presentation:
  - Immediate onset of dermal, ocular, and respiratory pain. Five minutes after
    exposure, the skin develops grayish areas of devitalized epithelium that progress
    to erythema within 30 min. Painful bullae develop in 2–3 hr and take up to 18 hr
    to fully develop.
  - Initial ocular symptoms include pain, instant blepharospasm, and conjunctival
    irritation progressing to edema of the conjunctiva, cornea (with clouding), iris,
    and lids. Eyes may be swollen shut within 1 hr.
  - Respiratory symptoms begin with instant and intense nasal and upper airway
    irritation, producing nasal and sinus burning, epistaxis, sore throat, laryngitis,
    vocal cord paralysis, and cough. Symptoms progress to necrotizing tracheobron-
    chitis with prominent pseudomembrane formation. Chemical pneumonitis,
    pulmonary edema, and respiratory failure may occur in severe cases, and are
    more common with lewisite than with mustard exposure.
  - Lewisite may also produce an increase in systemic capillary permeability with
    extravasation of intravascular fluids, hypovolemia, renal and/or hepatic necrosis,
    and shock.

DIAGNOSIS[3,37]
- History of exposure to an irritating gas and clinical presentation
- Leukocytosis on CBC is common and nonspecific.
- Reduced PaO_2 on ABG
- Chemical pneumonitis or noncardiogenic pulmonary edema on CXR

TREATMENT[3,37]
- Patient's skin must be decontaminated as soon as possible with 1 part bleach in 9 parts
  water, or soap and water. This should be done prior to arrival at the treatment facility.
- Patients with mild, nonproductive cough, nasal irritation, and/or sore throat that
  began more than 12 hr after exposure may be sent home with cough medication,
  throat lozenges, and instructions to use a cool steam vaporizer.[42]
- Initiate fluid replacement with colloids and/or crystalloids as needed.

- BAL (British anti-lewisite, dimercaprol): 3 mg/kg deep IM injection Q 4 hr for 2 days only in severe, life-threatening exposures. Read package insert carefully for contraindications and complications.
- Antibiotic ophthalmic ointment or petroleum jelly should be applied to the edges of the eyelids at least qid to prevent adhesions.
- Culture damaged skin and pulmonary secretions often.
- Control bronchospasm, if present, with theophylline, albuterol, and IV steroids.
- Provide oxygen, intubation, mechanical ventilation, and PEEP or CPAP as necessary. If intubation seems likely, it should be performed early before laryngeal spasm and edema make it too difficult or impossible.

ISOLATION PRECAUTIONS   Victims should be decontaminated prior to arrival at the treatment facility. Further decontamination, if needed, can be performed with 1 part bleach and 9 parts water, or soap and water, while wearing appropriate protective gear. Otherwise, use standard precautions (gloves, hand washing, and splash precautions, as needed).

A Detailed Quick Reference for

Phosgene Oxime (CX)

OVERVIEW[3,37,38]   Phosgene oxime is often incorrectly classified as a vesicant (mustard, lewisite), but it is actually an urticant producing skin wheals instead of blisters. Phosgene oxime exists as a solid below 95°F (35°C) but has a high vapor pressure, allowing for significant offgassing. The solid form is a colorless crystal, and the liquid form is yellowish brown with a strong, unpleasant odor. In a terrorist attack, it would likely be released as a liquid aerosol or vapor and has an LD_{50} of about 25 mg/kg for skin exposure. It is a strong corrosive and irritant and tends to produce more severe tissue damage than the vesicants.

LATENT PERIOD   The latent period is characterized by the immediate onset of severe pain and irritation of all exposed skin and mucous membranes, with erythema and wheal formation in 30 min and tissue necrosis in 24 hr.

SYMPTOMS AND CLINICAL COURSE[3,37,42]
- Initial presentation:
  - Immediate onset of severe dermal, ocular, and respiratory pain. The dermis demonstrates areas of blanching with an erythematous ring within 30 seconds of exposure, progressing to wheal formation in 30 min. Skin necrosis develops in about 24 hr after exposure.
  - Initial ocular symptoms, in even mild exposures, include intense pain, redness, lacrimation, blepharospasm, and lid edema. Higher exposures can produce iritis, corneal clouding, ulceration or perforation, and blindness.
  - Respiratory symptoms begin with nasal and upper airway irritation, producing nasal and sinus burning, sore throat, laryngitis, and cough. They may progress to necrosis and sloughing of the airway mucosa. Chemical pneumonitis, pulmonary edema, and respiratory failure are more common with phosgene oxime than with the vesicants and may begin to develop several hours after exposure.

DIAGNOSIS[3,37]
- History of exposure to an irritating gas and clinical presentation
- There are no specific diagnostic tests for phosgene oxime.
- Reduced PaO_2 on ABG
- Chemical pneumonitis or noncardiogenic pulmonary edema on CXR

TREATMENT[3,37]
- Patient's contaminated clothing should be removed, and the skin must be decontaminated as soon as possible with soap and water. This should be done prior to arrival at the treatment facility.
- Patients with skin or eye lesions or with respiratory symptoms should be admitted. Patients with large dermal burns or dyspnea should be admitted to the ICU. Patients with lesser symptoms should be observed for at least 6 hr before discharge.[42]
- Initiate fluid replacement with colloids and/or crystalloids as needed.
- Administer ophthalmic antibiotics and arrange early ophthalmologic consultation.

- Control bronchospasm, if present, with theophylline and albuterol.
- Provide oxygen, intubation, mechanical ventilation, and PEEP or CPAP as necessary. If intubation seems likely, it should be performed early before laryngeal spasm and edema make it too difficult or impossible.

ISOLATION PRECAUTIONS   Victims should be decontaminated prior to arrival at the treatment facility. Further decontamination, if needed, can be performed with soap and water, while wearing appropriate protective gear. Otherwise, use standard precautions (gloves, hand washing, and splash precautions, as needed).

A Detailed Quick Reference for

Anhydrous Ammonia, Sulfur Dioxide, and Hydrogen Chloride

OVERVIEW[38,42,43] Anhydrous ammonia, sulfur dioxide, and hydrogen chloride are all gases and exert their major toxicity via inhalation and direct contact. They all have similar effects on living tissue and produce consequences similar to both vesicants and pulmonary agents. They may be classified as tissue corrosive agents.

Anhydrous ammonia (NH_3) is a colorless, lighter than air, extremely irritating gas with a strong suffocating odor. When it comes in contact with the moisture of mucous membranes, it forms the strong corrosive ammonium hydroxide (NH_4OH). **Sulfur dioxide** (SO_2) is a colorless, heavier than air, severely irritating gas with a pungent sulfur odor. When it comes in contact with the moisture of mucous membranes, it forms the strong corrosive sulfurous acid (H_2SO_3). **Hydrogen chloride** (HCl, hydrochloric acid) is a colorless to yellowish gas that forms a heavier than air corrosive vapor on contact with air.

Toxic exposure to all these agents occurs by inhalation and contact with the eyes, skin, and mucous membranes, where they quickly produce severe chemical burns. They have many industrial and agricultural uses and may be stored in large quantities. In high exposures, the effects of these agents on the respiratory system are similar to those of the pulmonary agents, except that their onset (latent period) is much shorter in comparison.

LATENT PERIOD The latent period is seconds to minutes, depending on the level of exposure.

SYMPTOMS AND CLINICAL COURSE[38,42,43]
- Initial presentation:
  - Based on upper airway, ocular and mucous membrane irritation, and consists of severe eye pain and conjunctival redness, lacrimation, sore throat, nasal irritation, sneezing, rhinorrhea, and coughing. These effects occur even at low exposures. At higher exposures, there may be chest tightness, nausea, vomiting, dyspnea, wheezing, tachycardia, cyanosis, and airway obstruction due to sloughed epithelium, edema, and bronchospasm. Laryngospasm and swelling may also lead to acute obstruction and asphyxia. High levels of exposure may produce severe chemical pneumonitis and pulmonary edema. Lung damage may be permanent.
  - Ocular symptoms include conjunctival irritation progressing to keratoconjunctivitis, with sloughing of the superficial tissues of the eye, ulcers, perforation, and temporary or permanent blindness.
  - Dermal symptoms include immediate severe skin irritation with a stinging pain, erythema, and blistering in areas exposed to these chemicals. Deep burns and skin necrosis, especially in moist areas, are not uncommon.

DIAGNOSIS[38,42,43] There are no specific diagnostic tests for these agents.
- History of exposure to an irritating gas and symptoms at presentation
- Reduced PaO_2 on ABG

- CXR may initially be normal and can take up to 48 hr to demonstrate chemical pneumonitis or noncardiogenic pulmonary edema.

TREATMENT[38,42,43]   There is no specific treatment or antidote.
- Initiate oxygen therapy and supportive care.
- Control airway and manage airway secretions and dead tissue.
- Control bronchospasm, if present, with theophylline and albuterol.
- Provide intubation, mechanical ventilation, and PEEP as necessary. Early intubation may be necessary, especially in children.

ISOLATION PRECAUTIONS   Decontamination is usually not needed, although wet clothing should be cautiously removed, as all of these agents readily dissolve in water. Use standard precautions (gloves, hand washing, and splash precautions, as needed).

A Detailed Quick Reference for

Hydrogen Fluoride

OVERVIEW[38,42,43]   Hydrogen fluoride (HF, hydrofluoric acid) is a colorless, lighter than air, fuming liquid or gas with a strong, irritating odor. Toxicity occurs by inhalation of the gas, fumes or aerosol, and by contact of the gas or liquid with skin, eyes and mucous membranes. Hydrogen fluoride is a tissue corrosive agent similar in its effects to anhydrous ammonia (NH_3), sulfur dioxide (SO_2), and hydrogen chloride (HCl, hydrochloric acid). Its fluoride ion, once absorbed, can also produce serious or fatal systemic toxic affects, even at low doses.

LATENT PERIOD   Local effects are immediate, but pulmonary effects may be immediate or delayed for 12–36 hr. Systemic effects may take days to appear, depending on the level of exposure.

SYMPTOMS AND CLINICAL COURSE[38,42,43]
- Initial presentation:
  - Respiratory symptoms include sore throat, nasal irritation, sneezing, rhinorrhea, and coughing. Severe effects include chest tightness, dyspnea, wheezing, tachycardia, cyanosis, and airway obstruction due to laryngospasm and swelling. Lung injury may appear quickly or be delayed for 12–36 hr. Symptoms include chemical pneumonitis, pulmonary edema, and collapsed lung and may occur even following only skin exposure. Lung injury may be permanent.
  - Ocular symptoms include immediate onset of eye pain, lacrimation, conjunctival irritation progressing to keratoconjunctivitis, with sloughing of the superficial tissues of the eye, ulcers, perforation, and temporary or permanent blindness.
  - Dermal symptoms include immediate severe skin irritation and pain, erythema and blistering in exposed areas, deep burns, and skin necrosis. Hydrogen fluoride solutions in concentrations of 20–50% can produce pain and swelling that is delayed by up to 8 hr following exposure.
  - Systemic effects from exposure by any route include nausea, vomiting, abdominal pain, and cardiac arrhythmias due to severe calcium, potassium, and magnesium imbalances.
    - Hypocalcemia: this can be severe and lead to tetany, seizures, reduced cardiac contractility, and cardiovascular collapse.
    - Hyperkalemia: this can be severe and lead to paresthesias, weakness, paralysis, abnormal EKG, and cardiac standstill.
    - Hypomagnesemia: this can be severe and lead to serious cardiac arrhythmias.

DIAGNOSIS[38,42,43]   There are no specific diagnostic tests for hydrogen fluoride.
- History of exposure to an irritating gas and symptoms at presentation
- Hypocalcemia, hyperkalemia, and/or hypomagnesemia are suggestive.
- CXR initially may be normal and can take up to 48 hr to demonstrate chemical pneumonitis or noncardiogenic pulmonary edema.

TREATMENT[38,42,43]   There is no specific treatment or antidote.

- Initiate oxygen therapy and supportive care.
- Monitor serial EKGs and serum calcium, magnesium, and potassium levels.
- Treat burns with a calcium gluconate gel (2.5 g calcium gluconate in 100 ml K-Y jelly) 4–5 times a day for 3–4 days.
- In inhalational exposures, give nebulized 2.5% calcium gluconate (1.5 ml 10% calcium gluconate in 4.5 ml NS) to limit further systemic fluoride absorption from the lungs.
- Treat hypocalcemia with 10% calcium gluconate 0.1–0.2 mL/kg, up to 10 ml over 2–3 min.
- Treat hypomagnesemia with 2–4 ml of 50% magnesium sulfate over 40–60 min.
- Treat hypokalemia, hypotension, and cardiac arrhythmias in the usual manner.
- Control bronchospasm with theophylline and albuterol (racemic epinephrine in children).
- Provide intubation, mechanical ventilation, and PEEP as necessary. Early intubation may be necessary, especially in children.

ISOLATION PRECAUTIONS   Decontamination is usually not needed for gas or vapor exposure. Any liquid hydrogen fluoride or wet clothing should be cautiously removed while wearing appropriate personal protective equipment. Use standard precautions (gloves, hand washing, and splash precautions, as needed).

A Detailed Quick Reference for

Arsine

OVERVIEW[38,42,43] Arsine (AsH_3) is a colorless, heavier than air, nonirritating gas with a slight garlic or fishy odor. It is the most toxic form of arsenic. Exposure is by inhalation and absorption through the lungs, and as little as 3 ppm is a toxic dose. It produces no immediate effects or symptoms to warn of exposure. Arsine's major toxic effect is to enter red blood cells and produce an acute intravascular hemolysis. Mortality is about 25% following acute exposure. Arsine has many uses in industry, especially in the manufacture of computer chips and fiberoptics.

LATENT PERIOD The latent period is 2–24 hr following exposure.

SYMPTOMS AND CLINICAL COURSE[38,42,43]
- Initial presentation:
    - Nausea, vomiting, crampy abdominal pain, malaise, dizziness, headache, dyspnea, and occasionally paresthesias and delirium.
    - Hemolysis begins 2–24 hr after exposure and may continue for up to 96 hr. This can produce dyspnea, hypotension, hyperkalemia with consistent EKG changes, and hypocalcemia.
    - Red staining of the conjunctiva may be an early sign.
    - Late effects include renal failure from acute tubular necrosis due to severe hemoglobinuria, hepatomegaly, and jaundice.

DIAGNOSIS[38,42,43] There are no specific diagnostic tests for arsine.
- A CBC will usually show anemia and the products of hemolysis (irregular RBC sizes and shapes and RBC fragments). Plasma-free hemoglobin will usually be elevated.
- Coombs' tests and RBC fragility tests are usually normal.
- Chemistry tests may demonstrate an elevated serum potassium, BUN, creatinine, and liver enzymes. Hypocalcemia may also be present.

TREATMENT[38,42,43] There is no specific treatment or antidote.
- Provide oxygen therapy by mask and supportive care.
- Monitor serial serum electrolytes, BUN, creatinine, calcium, and HCT.
- Avoid fluid overload in case of impending renal failure, and consider treatment of hypotension with dopamine.
- Treat hemoglobinuria with urinary alkalinization (50–100 mEq sodium bicarbonate in 1 L of D5 0.25% NS at a rate to maintain a urine output of 2–3 ml/kg/hr, with a urine pH > 7.5.
- Send blood early for type and cross, as an exchange transfusion may become necessary.
- **Do not use chelating agents, as they are ineffective in arsine, even when used early.**

ISOLATION PRECAUTIONS Decontamination is usually not necessary. Use standard precautions (gloves, hand washing, and splash precautions, as needed).

A Detailed Quick Reference for

Lacrimators (Tear Gas)

OVERVIEW[3,37,38]   **CN** (Chloroacetophenone), also known as mace, **CS** (orthochloro-benzylidene malononitrile), and **CR** (dibenoxazepine) are the tear gas agents in most common use today for riot control. As opposed to most other chemical weapons, these agents tend to be particulate solids at normal ambient temperatures and are usually released as a smoke or mist. In some terrorist situations, they could be released and initially claimed to be a vesicant or pulmonary agent in an attempt to create panic. **The clinical presentation of the lacrimators differs from that of the vesicants, pulmonary agents, and tissue corrosive agents in that the onset of symptoms is immediate but will improve in 15–30 min following termination of exposure to the lacrimators, whereas symptom onset may be delayed and will continue to worsen for hours to days following the termination of exposure to the other agents.**

LATENT PERIOD   The latent period is seconds.

SYMPTOMS AND CLINICAL COURSE[3,37,38]
- Initial presentation:
  - Lacrimation, conjunctival redness, blepharospasm, burning, and irritation of the eyes, nose, mouth, and throat, rhinorrhea, sneezing, salivation, cough, bronchorrhea, chest tightness, and tingling or burning and erythema of the skin.
  - Pulmonary function tests following exposure will usually be normal or show no change from the patient's baseline values.
  - Eye and respiratory symptoms usually spontaneously resolve 15–30 min after the termination of exposure, and skin pain and erythema subside 45–60 min after the termination of exposure.
  - Rarely, there may be severe erythema and vesicle formation (similar to a second-degree burn) beginning hours after a very high exposure at high ambient temperatures and humidity.

DIAGNOSIS[3,37,38]
- There are no specific diagnostic tests, and the diagnosis is based on history, presentation, and clinical course.

TREATMENT[3,37,38]
- No specific treatment is required.
- Patients who have not received decontamination prior to arrival at the treatment facility should remove clothing and store it in a plastic bag until laundered.
- Skin can be decontaminated with 1 part bleach in 9 parts water, or with soap and water.
- Eyes may be flushed with saline or water.

ISOLATION PRECAUTIONS   If decontamination is necessary, it should be performed outside the treatment facility or in a dedicated decontamination room using at least level C protection. Use standard precautions (gloves, hand washing, and splash precautions, as needed).

References

1   Mandell, Douglas, Bennett. *Principles and Practice of Infectious Diseases.* 5th ed. New York: Churchill Livingstone; 2000.
2. Sidell, Patrick, Dashiell. *Jane's Chem-Bio Handbook.* Jane's Information Group; 1999.
3. *PDR Guide to Biological and Chemical Warfare Response.* Thomson/Physician Desk Reference; 2002.
4. Alibek K. *Biohazard.* Dell Publishing; 1999.
5. Eitzen E, Paulin J, Cieslak T, et al. *Medical Management of Biological Casualties Handbook (The Blue Book).* U.S. Army Institute of Infectious Disease (USAMRIID). July, 1998.
6. Centers for Disease Control and Prevention (CDC) Bioterrorism Web site. Available at: http://www.bt.cdc.gov.
7. Fenner F, Henderson DA, et al. *Smallpox and Its Eradication.* WHO; 1968.
8. Mounts AW, Arita I, Kaur H, Parashar UD, et al. A cohort study of health care workers to assess nosocomial transmissibility of Nipah virus, Malaysia, 1999. *J Infect Dis.* 2001;183(5): 810–813.
9. Amal NM, Lyems, Ksiazek TG, et al. Risk factors for the Nipah virus transmission, Port Dickson, Negeri Sembilan, Malaysia: Results from a hospital-based case-control study. *Southeast Asian J Trop Med Public Health.* 2000;31(2):301–306.
10. Chua KB, Lam SK, Goh KJ, et al. The presence of Nipah virus in respiratory secretions and urine of patients during an outbreak of Nipah virus encephalitis in Malaysia. *J Infect.* 2001;42(1):40–43.
11. Chong HT, Kamaralzaman A, Tan CT, et al. Treatment of acute Nipah encephalitis with ribavirin. *Ann Neurol.* 2001;49(6): 810–813.
12. Crameri G, Wang LF, Morrissy C, et al. A rapid immune plaque assay for the detection of Hendra and Nipah viruses and anti-virus antibodies. *J Virol Methods.* 2002;99(1–2):41–51.
13. Nijjar MS, Nijjar SS. Domoic acid–induced neurodegeneration resulting in memory loss is mediated by Ca2+ overload and inhibition of Ca2+ calmodulin-stimulated adenylate cyclase in rat brain [review]. *Int J Mol Med.* 2000;6(4):377–389.
14. *Amnesic Shellfish Poisoning (ASP).* HAB Publication Series Vol. 1, Intergovernmental Oceanographic Commission, Manuals and Guides No. 31, Vol. 1. UNESCO; 1995.
15. North Atlantic Treaty Organization (NATO). *The Medical Aspects of NBC Defensive Operations AmedP-6(B): Potential Biological Agent Operational Data Charts* FM 8-9.
16. Tetrodotoxin poisoning associated with eating puffer fish transported from Japan—California, 1996. *MMWR.* May 17, 1996;389–391.
17. Lang WR. Puffer fish poisoning. *Am Fam Physician.* 1990;42:1029–1033.
18. *Chemical and Biological Terrorism: Research and Development to Improve Civilian Medical Response.* Institute of Medicine and National Academy Press; 1999.
19. *Planning Guidance for the Health System Response to a Bioevent in the National Capital Region.* Washington, DC: Metropolitan Washington Council of Governments; 2001.
20. Garner JS. Guidelines for infection control practices in hospitals. *Infect Control Hosp Epidemiol.* 1996;17:53–60.
21. Inglesby TV, O'Toole T, Henderson DA, et al. Anthrax as a biological weapon 2002: Updated recommendations for management. *JAMA.* 2002;287(17):2236–2252.
22. Borio L, Inglesby T, Peters CJ, et al. Hemorrhagic fever viruses as biological weapons, medical and public health management. *JAMA.* 2002;297(18):2391–2405.
23. Strickland GT, ed. *Hunter's Tropical Medicine and Emerging Infectious Diseases.* 8th ed. Philadelphia: WB Saunders; 2000.
24. Aflatoxins. In: *Foodborne Pathogenic Microorganisms and Natural Toxins Handbook (Bad Bug Book).* FDA/CFSAN; September, 1998.

25. Investigation of bioterrorism-related anthrax and interim guidelines for exposure management and antimicrobial therapy. *MMWR.* October 26, 2001;50:909–919.

26. Jernigan JA, Stephens DS, Ashford DA, et al. Bioterrorism-related inhalational anthrax: the first 10 cases reported in the United States. *Emerging Infect Dis.* 2001;7(6)

27. Chikungunya fever among U.S. Peace Corps volunteers: Republic of the Philippines. *MMWR.* September 12, 1986;573–574.

28. Meeting report: Symposium on Marburg and Ebola Viruses. *Virus Res.* 2001;80:117–123.

29. Russell P, Eley SM, Ellis J et al. Comparison of efficacy of ciprofloxacin and doxycycline against experimental melioidosis and glanders. *J Antimicrob Chemother.* 2000;45(6):813–818.

30. Graziano KI, Tempest B. Hantavirus pulmonary syndrome: a zebra worth knowing. *Am Fam Physician.* September 15, 2002;1015–1020.

31. Influenza. World Health Organization Fact Sheet 211. February 1999.

32. Influenza A (H5N1). World Health Organization Fact Sheet 188. January 1998.

33. Olsnes S, Refsnes K, Pihl A, et al. Mechanism of action of the toxic lectins abrin and ricin. *Nature.* 1974;249:627–631.

34. Balint GA. Ricin: the toxic protein of castor oil seeds. *Toxicology.* 1974;2:77–102.

35. Epidemiologic notes and reports paralytic shellfish poisoning: Massachusetts and Alaska, 1990. *MMWR.* March 15, 1991;157–161.

36. Dennis DT, Inglesby TV, Henderson DA, et al. Tularemia as a biological weapon. *JAMA.* 2001;285(21):2763.

37. *Medical Management of Chemical Casualties Handbook.* 3rd ed. Chemical Casualty Care Division, USAMRICD; 1998.

38. Goldfrank LR, Flourenbaum NF, Lewin NA, et al. *Goldfrank's Toxicologic Emergencies.* 7th ed. New York: McGraw-Hill; 2002.

39. Sidell FR, Borak J. Chemical warfare agents, II: nerve agents. *Ann Emerg Med.* July 1992;21:865–871.

40. Holstege CP, Kirk M, Sidell FR, et al. Chemical warfare: nerve agent poisoning. *Med Toxicol.* 1997;13(4):923–942.

41. De Lorenzo RA, Porter RS. *Weapons of Mass Destruction Emergency Care.* Prentice Hall Health; 2000.

42. Agency for Toxic Substances and Disease Registry (Department of Health and Human Services). *Managing Hazardous Material Incidents.* 2001.

43. Gosselin RE, Smith RP, Hodge HC, et al. *Clinical Toxicology of Commercial Products.* 5th ed. Baltimore: Williams and Wilkins; 1984.

Glossary

The glossary is provided for non–healthcare providers and non–medical first responders who may require the use of this book.

ABG: arterial blood gases
adenopathy: the presence of lymph nodes
amox-clav: amoxicillin-clavulanate
anorexia: loss of appetite
ARDS: acute respiratory distress syndrome
arrhythmia: an abnormal heartbeat rhythm
arthralgias: joint pains
ASA: acetylsalicylic acid (aspirin)
AsH₃: arsine
asthenia: loss of strength
ataxia: jerky movements and unsteady gait
BAL: British anti-lewisite
bleeding diathesis: the tendency to bleed excessively
blepharospasm: involuntary tight closing of the eyelids
bradycardia: abnormally slow heartbeat
bronchorrhea: the production of excess mucus or phlegm in the airways
BUN: blood urea nitrogen
CAT: computerized axial tomography
CBC: complete blood count
CCHF: Crimean-Congo hemorrhagic fever
CDC: Centers for Disease Control and Prevention
CNS: central nervous system
CPAP: continuous positive airway pressure
CPK: creatine phosphokinase
CPR: cardiopulmonary resuscitation
CSF: cerebrospinal fluid
CXR: chest x-ray
demyelinating: destruction of a myelin sheath that covers most nerves
DHF: dengue hemorrhagic fever
diaphoresis: sweating
DIC: disseminated intravascular coagulation; many tiny blood clots forming within the circulating blood
diplopia: double vision
dysesthesia: altered or unpleasantly distorted sense of touch
dysphagia: difficulty swallowing
dysphonia: difficulty speaking
dyspnea: shortness of breath
EEE: Eastern equine encephalitis
EKG: electrocardiogram
ELISA: enzyme linked immunosorbent assay
epigastric: pertaining to the mid upper abdomen
epistaxis: nosebleed

ER: emergency room

erythema: redness

eschar: a hard scab

etiology: the cause of a specific disease

FFP: fresh frozen plasma

FLI: flulike illness

fomites: any object or item that can become contaminated by touch and transmit an infectious organism

GI: gastrointestinal

H and E: hematoxylin and eosin

HCT: hematocrit

hematemesis: vomiting blood

hematochezia: red blood in the stool (as opposed to black blood in the stool, which is called melena)

hematogenous: via the bloodstream

hematuria: blood in the urine

hemoglobinuria: the presence of free hemoglobin in the urine

hemolysis: the bursting of red blood cells

hemoptysis: coughing up blood (blood in the sputum or phlegm)

hepatosplenomegaly: enlarged liver and spleen

HFRS: Hemorrhagic fever with renal syndrome

hilar adenopathy: the presence of lymph nodes in the chest noted on chest x-ray or CAT scan

HPS: Hantavirus pulmonary syndrome

hyperkalemia: an abnormally elevated level of potassium in the blood

hypocalcemia: an abnormally reduced level of calcium in the blood

hypomagnesemia: an abnormally reduced level of magnesium in the blood

hyporeflexia: reduced reflexes

ICU: intensive care unit

IDCF: immunodiffusion-complement-fixation

IDTP: immunodiffusion-tube-precipitin

IFA: indirect fluorescent antibody

IHA: indirect hemagglutination assay

ILI: influenza-like illness

IM: intramuscular

IV: intravenous, intravenously

IVP: intravenous pyelogram, pyelography

jaundice: yellowing of the skin, usually due to liver problems

KOH: potassium hydroxide

LD$_{50}$: the dose of a toxin required to kill half the exposed victims

LFTs: liver function tests

LSD: lysergic acid diethylamide

lymphadenopathy: the presence of lymph nodes

maculopapular rash: a rash consisting of macules (flat lesions) and papules (small, hard, raised bumps)

malaise: a general feeling of unwellness

MAT: microscopic agglutination test

MIF: microimmunofluorescence

miosis: constricted pupils
MRI: magnetic resonance imaging
myalgia or myalgias: muscle pain
mydriasis: dilated pupils
myoclonus: sudden spasmodic jerking of the muscles
NACl: sodium chloride
NaHCO$_3$: sodium bicarbonate
necrosis: tissue death
NSAID: nonsteroidal anti-inflammatory drug
oliguria: reduced urinary output
papule: a small, hard, raised bump on the skin
paresthesias: tingling
PCR: polymerase chain reaction
PDR: *Physicians' Desk Reference*
PEEP: positive end-expiratory pressure
petechiae: tiny, round, red spots caused by bleeding into the skin
PFIB: perfluoroisobutylene
photophobia: excessive visual light sensitivity
PMN: polymorphonuclear neutrophil leukocytes
PPE: personal protective equipment
prostration: a feeling of helpless exhaustion
PO: by mouth, orally
proteinuria: protein in the urine
pruritic: itchy
ptosis: drooping eyelid(s)
PTT: partial thromboplastin time
pustule: a small pus-containing bump on the skin
RBC: red blood cell
rhinorrhea: runny nose
rigors: shaking chills (usually occurs as fever rises)
RMSF: Rocky Mountain spotted fever
SCBA: self-contained breathing apparatus
SEB: staphylococcal enterotoxin B
sepsis: an infection in the blood (also septicemia)
SI: sacroiliac
somnolence: drowsiness
SQ: subcutaneous
suppurative: producing abscesses, drainage, or pus
TB: tuberculosis
tenesmus: strong feeling of having to defecate without producing any stool
tetany: involuntary and often rigid muscle spasms and twitching
TMP-SMX: trimethoprim-sulfamethoxazol
toxemia: the presence of toxins in the blood
UV: ultraviolet
virion: individual virus particle
WBC: white blood cell
wheal: a temporary, raised area on the skin, like a hive
y.o.: years old

Index

Emboldened page numbers refer to discussion in the "Detailed Quick Reference" sections.